# A TRIDENT SCHOLAR
# PROJECT REPORT

NO. 218

---

THE "GREAT CODE" IN SHAKESPEARE'S HENRIAD

---

# UNITED STATES NAVAL ACADEMY
# ANNAPOLIS, MARYLAND

# ABSTRACT

Northrop Frye has proven to be one of the most important literary theorists of contemporary literary criticism. His literary theories, as presented in *Anatomy of Criticism* and *The Great Code*, have become bench-marks in Biblical literary criticism. In his book *The Great Code*, Frye argues that "Biblical imagery and narrative...had set up an imaginative framework -- a mythological universe -- within which Western literature had operated down to the eighteenth century and is to a large extent still operating." Frye shows how Biblical narrative has become, unconsciously, the context for Western understanding of narrative and imagery in art and literature. Specifically, Frye suggests that "the context of the Bible is traditionally described as typological "revelation" that "proceeds from the beginning to the end of its story" and exists in seven typological phases: creation, revolution (exodus), law, wisdom, prophecy, gospel, and apocalypse.

This research project tests Frye's theories about the influence of Biblical imagery and narrative on a masterpiece of Western art, Shakespeare's *Henriad* (*Richard II*, *Henry IV, Part I*, *Henry IV, Part II*, and *Henry V*). Although many literary critics have examined Shakespeare's use of the Bible "most of them catalogue the Biblical allusions without discussing their functions in the plays." This research focus on Shakespeare's use of the Bible in his drama, however, it investigates how his *Henriad* manifests "the great code" of Biblical narrative "revelation." Specifically, it examines how typological "revelation" gives meaning to the *Henriad*, his longest coherent dramatic effort, in the same manner as it does in the Bible: through myth and metaphor.

Finally, this project recognizes the inadequacies of Frye's typological phase model in extricating meaning from the *Henriad* and explores the realm of language to discover why.

Key Words: Bible, Shakespeare, Typology, Language

# TABLE OF CONTENTS

## INTRODUCTION: AN OVERVIEW

The title of this project, "The 'Great Code' in Shakespeare's *Henriad*," is slightly daunting at first sight, and requires some explanation. The "Great Code" refers to Northrop Frye's *The Great Code: the Bible and Literature.* Shakespeare's *Henriad*, as I use it, refers specifically to Shakespeare's second tetralogy of history plays *Richard II*, *Henry IV, Part 1*, *Henry IV, Part 2*, and *Henry V*.

Shakespeare wrote two historical tetralogies known as the first and second *Henriads*, respectively. The first *Henriad*, consisting of *Henry VI, Part 1*, *Henry VI, Part 2*, *Henry VI, Part 3*, and *Richard III*, was written early in Shakespeare's career as a dramatist, between 1589 and 1592, and is considered an immature work because of its verbal and dramatic inconsistencies, though it is still impressive. The second tetralogy, which is the focus of my research, was written by the more experienced playwright between the years 1595 and 1599; this is the masterpiece of a more mature Shakespeare who would soon compose his powerful tragedies in the early years of the 1600's. Although written earlier, the first tetralogy dramatizes the later years of the War of the Roses, between 1422-1485. The second tetralogy covers the years 1398-1422 in English history. The plays that make up each tetralogy were, in fact, written to stand alone; however, within each tetralogy, and even amongst the two tetralogies, the plays are historically and dramatically interconnected.

Northrop Frye, the literary critic, who developed the approach that I have used to examine Shakespeare's second *Henriad*, will probably be remembered as the twentieth century's greatest literary critic. His many works of criticism elude easy classification, but many critics "have tried to embalm [them] in a sarcophagus of 'myth criticism' unconnected with other types of criticism"[1]. The theory of literary classification that Frye sketched in his masterwork *Anatomy of Criticism* (1947) has provided the field of literary criticism with a vision, pointing in the direction of further clarification of what is an all too often enigmatic discipline. As my primary excavation tool for unearthing deeper meaning in Shakespeare's history plays, I am using one of Frye's more obscure works, which received less than unanimous acceptance by most contemporary literary critics. Although Frye acknowledged that *The Great Code* (1982) was, in places, "a very vulnerable work," its insight and understanding of how the Bible functions on the narrative level offers an innovative exploration of art that functions in the Biblical mode[2]. Frye's attempt in this book to find a "unity of narrative and imagery" in the Bible and Western literature provides a guiding vision for future Biblical literary criticism[3]. Despite Frye's foresight, however, "not everyone is prepared yet for such a paradigm shift" in the approach to literary criticism[4].

Beyond the reference to Northrop Frye's book, I apply the term "great code" in this project to Frye's "'great code' principle" which claims that "the organizing structures of the Bible and the corresponding structures of 'secular literature' reflect each other"[5]. From Frye's critical approach to understanding Biblical narrative, I have developed a specific method of Biblical, typological analysis that I have applied to Shakespeare's second *Henriad* to uncover a typological cycle that is subtly operating throughout the sequence of the *Henriad*. One might initially ask how I determined there was a "great code," or any "code," for that matter, operating in these plays. Furthermore, if there was a "code" in place, one might ask how I came to understand it. The answers to these question are complicated, and I will discuss them in greater detail in the main body of this paper. It is more important at this point, however, to provide an overview of the basic methodology that I used to deduce these answers. They ultimately have led me far beyond the "great code" in Shakespeare's *Henriad*, to an examination of the tendency of modern literary criticism to misunderstand language and to obscure meaning in art. Ultimately they have led me to a theory of language that seeks to understand how the creative imagination creates art through language.

Reading through the four plays of the second *Henriad*, I was struck by the occurrence of several peculiarities. The first oddity I noticed was that Shakespeare had altered the actual history that he was portraying in order to make these plays both more symmetrical and more metaphorical. Although he did factually trace the flow of history throughout the plays, he also made carefully tailored character alterations that affected the balance of the plays, such as making Hotspur and his father, Northumberland, a generation younger than they in fact were to serve as foils for Prince Hal and his father, Henry IV[6].

Edmund Mortimer is another example of Shakespeare's dramatic

mischaracterization of a historical figure. Shakespeare may not have realized

that his historical sources confused the infant Edmund Mortimer the fifth with

his uncle Sir Edmund Mortimer, conflating them into one person, but, as Saccio

suggests, "it is possible that...[Shakespeare] would have conflated the

Mortimers anyway," in order to create a dramatic balance between Hotspur and

Mortimer (Mortimer being the adult brother-in-law of Hotspur and the infant heir

to Richard's throne all rolled into one character)[7].

The significance of these changes can be seen either as "dramatic

expediency," as Peter Saccio explains it in his book *Shakespeare's English

Kings* (1977), or as dramatic genius[8]. By calling Shakespeare a dramatic

genius, I am not offering a cliché compliment to a dead poet, but rather

recognizing that Shakespeare understood the preeminence of dramatic effect

over historical fact. As a dramatist Shakespeare was more concerned about

the dramatic "truth" of his plays than their historical precision. My definition of

"truth," in this context, is the creation of a "transcendent fundamental or spiritual

reality" that relates to the human condition in a more telling manner than fact[9].

This realization was the first hint to me that Shakespeare was doing

much more with these plays than simply telling a factual story. His emphasis

on recreating a story in which the revelation of "truth" was paramount, even

over detailed "facts," was reminiscent of the mode of operation that the Bible uses to convey meaning. Although both Shakespeare's history plays and the Bible are "intimately bound up with history," neither can be "properly read as a history book" because both devalue fact and "depend on metaphor but do not become less 'real' or 'true' by doing so"[10].

While considering this idea, I noticed the numerous Biblical allusions that Shakespeare weaves throughout these plays, and I was led to a striking question: what function do these seemingly random Biblical allusions serve in the plays? In looking for an answer, I found an essay entitled "Shakespeare's use of Scripture," by Edna Moore Robinson, stating that "dozens of books and articles have been written on Shakespeare's use of the Bible, but most of them catalogue the biblical allusions without discussing their function in the plays"[11]. Robinson offered an explanation of the function of these allusions in the plays by examining how Shakespeare used "one passage at a time for direct and immediate effect"[12] She concluded that:

> The fact that Shakespeare cites only one passage at a time of course precludes his fashioning and altering a set of scriptural phrases into the forms necessary to build them into an allegory unified by some extra-scriptural conception...His simplicity and directness in making biblical allusions render such a complex molding still more impossible than piecing Scripture together into mosaics[13].

Despite Robinson's argument, it seemed too simple to say that when Shakespeare alludes to or quotes Scripture "it is the essential, the straightforward, commonly accepted meaning, that he *always* had in mind" [my italics][14]. The second *Henriad* is a complicated series of plays that operates on dramatically and historically complex levels, with kings falling from and rising to power like waves that crest and trough. To assume that Shakespeare, with his Elizabethan understanding of the link between God and king, simply used "one passage at a time for direct and immediate effect," is to miss much of the meaning in these plays[15].

Reading only *Richard II*, one can see that the Biblical imagery that Shakespeare employs is used precisely to build "an allegory unified by some extra-scriptural conceptions"[16]. The first, and perhaps most important of these conceptions, is that England was a new garden of Eden on earth that saw "a second fall of cursèd man" (R2.III.iv.75). But this notion of England as a "sea-wallèd garden" that has witnessed a fall of man (brought on by the evil deeds of God's representative on earth, the king, that must later be paid for, and repented for, by other kings), continues throughout every play of the second *Henriad*. Although it is not a simple or obvious cycle of imagery, if one pays close attention to it (as I hope to do in this paper) this garden of England experiences a fall of man; it suffers as "the blood of English[men]...manure[s] the ground;" and it watches an ascension and a holy marriage, finally becoming "the world's best garden" at the end of *Henry V* (R2.IV.i.137 & H5.V.Ep.7). Contrary to what Robinson believes is "impossible," this series of history plays transforms "a complex molding" of Scriptural references and allusions into Scriptural mosaics[17].

Realizing that the Biblical allusions and references used by Shakespeare in the *Henriad* function as a mosaic, I attempted to try to quantify the pattern of their operation in the plays. It was, as Robinson demonstrated, simple to show how individual pieces of Scripture could be used in a local context. Fitting many of these pieces into some kind of big puzzle that would bring order and coherence to their meaning, however, proved to be more challenging. The first place I looked to for guidance was the Bible, itself made up of complex literary patterns, cycles, and structures that defy easy clarification of meaning.

Creating a Scriptural mosaic that mimicked Biblical narrative, Shakespeare was inevitably indebted to the structure of Biblical narrative. I reasoned, therefore, that Shakespeare must have used, whether consciously or subconsciously, a structural pattern for these allusions, that was similar to the structure found in the Bible. If these allusions in Shakespeare's *Henriad* did operate in a Biblical mode, then specific techniques of Biblical criticism would be valid, and especially relevant, in understanding the patterns within this Scriptural mosaic to piece together new meaning in the four history plays taken as a whole.

In his book *The Great Code: The Bible and Literature* (1982), Northrop Frye did most of the groundwork to fit the pieces of this Scriptural puzzle together by illustrating the structural pattern in Biblical narrative and giving some examples of the reproduction of this pattern in Western literature. Frye's efforts, however, focus mainly on the Bible and do not address Shakespeare's *Henriad*. The focus of this project, therefore, is to apply Frye's theory to the

*Henriad* to test for similar Biblical narrative patterns and analyze their function. From *The Great Code*, I specifically incorporated three of Frye's main ideas into my search for Biblical narrative patterns and my analysis of the function of the Scriptural mosaic in the second *Henriad*. The first was that Biblical narrative functions typologically in the revelation of its story from beginning to end. Typology is a means of understanding the Bible by seeing the events in the Old Testament as "types" or figures of the events in the New Testament which are "antitypes."[18]. An example of a "type" would be the covenant of the Jewish people in the Old Testament for which the life of Christ, in the New Testament, was the fulfillment of God's promise becoming an "antitype"[19].

The second idea that I borrowed from Frye's works was that of the relationship of typology to history. Because I was examining Shakespeare's History plays, it was important that I establish a theory of History in order to comprehend how Shakespeare understood history, both in his day and in his drama. Only after reading Frye's ideas about history, however, did I realize why his "great code" could be used to understand both a passage of Biblical narrative and a Shakespearian history play.

Typology assumes that specific "events" in time are of fundamental importance in determining meaning. These "events" only reveal meaning, however, when they appear in "type-antitype" pairs, each "type" and "antitype" being separated by a forward motion in time. This means that out of the millions of "events" that we experience every day, we can only place meaning

11

after we have recognized a pattern, in time, of significant events; this inevitably links typology to history. Art, literature and drama function typologically by using images and metaphors as "events" from which meaning is established by creating patterns of "type-antitype" pairs that make up motifs.

There are various ideas of history; typology helps us define one possible method of understanding. The particular method of history I wish to consider is a form of narrative history that I call historical narrative, which uses story telling to relate history. Historical narrative is different than the modern notion of history, because it downplays fact and relies on typology to ascribe meaning. The modern notion views history as both "a chronological record of significant events" and "an explanation of their causes"[20]. Typology, as Frye describes it, only deals with "significant events" which are important in establishing meaning in historical narrative. Frye alludes to the fact that the modern notion of history uses a process known as "causality" to locate meaning, which deals with "explanations of...causes." Causality assigns meaning by "searching for...preceding causes" to the millions of everyday "events" we experience[21]. It links "cause to effect" in a "verbal progression" that moves forward; however, the "mental operations preceding the writing out of the causal sequence move backward" in time, starting with effect and then searching for cause[22]. "Scientific or philosophic procedure," that involves examining the past for cause, operates in the causal mode.

The final point from Frye that I used in my analysis of the Scriptural mosaic in the History plays was his assertion that the patterns of typological revelation in the Bible follow a multi-phase cycle proceeding from creation, through revolution or exodus, law, wisdom, prophecy, and gospel, to apocalypse[23]. Each phase of revelation flows from type to antitype, at which point the phase changes and the antitype becomes a new type. The next phase then continues when this new type flows to a new antitype and is transformed into a new phase[24].

I find myself asking, at this point, "What does all this mean?" Simply put, Frye indicates that the Bible functions typologically, that the reader understands historical narrative through typology, and that a multi-stage typological pattern operates in Biblical narrative. This means, based on what I deduced above, that the Scriptural mosaic in the narrative of Shakespeare's history plays should operate in a similar pattern to the Biblical narrative. *The Great Code* primarily deals with the operation of Biblical typology; however in his next book, *Words with Power* (1990), Frye shows that "Western literature had operated down to the eighteenth century, and is to a large extent still operating" within narrative structures that are based on the "imaginative framework" that the Bible has imprinted on the Western imagination[25].

Frye's theory breaks down, however, when it is confronted with assigning Biblical, typological phases to specific passages of Western literary narrative because he vaguely defines a criterion or method of classification for the phases of typology. His endeavor, in both *The Great Code* and *Words with*

*Power*, however, was to look beyond specifics, in order to establish broad guidelines which could be applied to a larger coherent literary theory. The development of a specific method that would test Frye's theory on a piece of Western art, such as the *Henriad*, was left to me.

Taking Frye's descriptions of each typological phase as a starting point, I established a criterion to classify narrative passages containing Biblical allusions and quotations. I slowly pieced together a method that categorized the narrative passages according to their function in the plays. My next task was to find and classify these narrative passages in the plays in order to trace the cycle of the Scriptural mosaic through the *Henriad*. This was, by far, the most tedious task of the project. It required extreme precision to locate the typological "nodes," points within the plays that corresponded exactly with a certain type or antitype within a certain phase. Because art cannot be simply boiled down to a fish-bone-like structure of meaning, however, it was impossible at times to locate nodes that had exact correspondence with their phase. In these instances, I was required to discriminate accurately between passages that were close to a node, but ultimately not exactly in one.

Fortunately for artists, and unfortunately for literary critics, art cannot be reduced to quick and easy "bullets" or "sound bites" of meaning. Good art typically eludes easy clarification of meaning, which is certainly true in the case of Shakespeare's second *Henriad*. The fact that I could not quite make an exact fit of the typological, narrative structure that I developed with the

14

Scriptural mosaic in Shakespeare's *Herriad* is a perfect example of how art escapes the tendency of the literary critic to box it neatly up. At this point we must make some distinctions between artist and critic in order to judge both the value and the limitations of the critical approach that I have developed from the works of Northrop Frye.

Where it is artist's role to recreate meaning in his art, it is the critic's function to extricate that meaning; or, at least, this is the ideal situation. Northrop Frye points out, however, that most modern criticism, which is made up of many extra-literary "schools" of criticism (new-criticism, historical, new-historical, structuralist, deconstructionist, psychological, feminist, Marxist, Freudian, etc...), is more concerned with forming "an interlocking body of mutual argument," that lacks "a larger perspective...of coherence for criticism as a whole"[26]. Unfortunately, "the bewildering number of new critical theories that have developed" in the last two decades has done much to obscure any critical coherence that previously existed[27].

The true victim of this movement in literary criticism has been the work, itself, which has undergone psycho-analysis, dissection, amputation, and mutilation. What is left of a work after the scientific operation that modern literary criticism performs on it is meaninglessness. The reason for this change is largely due to the fact that "the main focus of criticism [has] shifted from the poet to the reader"[28]. The reader, now having "an exaggerated and quite unrealistic importance," has the outrageous prerogative of taking a work out of context, ignoring altogether the poet who wrote it and obscuring any meaning, subtle or obvious, that it once had[29].

The critical approach I have taken in this paper is out of favor with modern literary criticism precisely because I am searching for meaning in a work that has a context, considering the influences on the poet and his background, and seeking to clarify the meaning of the work of art. But then again, I am using Northrop Frye, who has outrageously suggested to a literary critical community that "normally excludes [the Bible] from discussions of literature" that the Bible has fundamentally "influenced Western imagination," as a starting point for my analysis[30]. The method of typological criticism which is central to my analysis, has also been overly simplified and mislabeled by many critics who dismiss it as "Christian interpretation"[31]. David Bevington, editor of *The Complete Works of Shakespeare*, describes typological criticism of Shakespeare as a "controversy" surrounding the question, "Do the images and allusions of Shakespeare's plays show him to be deeply immersed in a Christian culture inherited from the Middle Ages?"[32]. To anyone one who has read any play by Shakespeare this question is not only obvious, but moot. To contest that Shakespeare was influenced by the cultural background of the Middle Ages reaches beyond absurdity and into ignorance. While "nobody would attempt to study Islamic culture without starting with the Koran, or Hindu culture without starting with Vedas and Upanishades," that is precisely what modern criticism seeks to do with Western literature and the Bible[33].

Yet modern criticism is not only opposed to finding meaning in a work of literature as a whole, some factions of criticism also completely dismiss the language out of which it is created. Deconstruction insists that "language is a system of difference--one in which the signifiers (such as words and gestures) are essentially arbitrary to the extent that 'meaning' and 'authorial intention' are virtually impossible to fix precisely; that is language enjoys a personal subjectivity"[34]. This follows directly from a critical approach in which the reader is the most important element in the interaction amongst the objective work, subjective reader, and transcendental words and ideas (which a deconstructionist would claim have no "transcendental" meaning at all because their definitions are arbitrary). What results is an approach to literature which "proclaims that there is no single identifiable author in the traditional sense; instead of a single text, we have a potentially infinite number of texts"[35]. Ultimately this means that a text and the words that it is composed of are meaningless, and if this is the case, why should we bother studying it, or any other piece of literature, for that matter?

My application of Frye's typological approach to Shakespeare's *Henriad* is certainly an external construct. I am superimposing this construct on the plays to extract meaning. In this way it is no different than--say--a Marxist or Freudian approach. Yet, I will argue that my approach is more germane to the field of literature than that of extra-literary approaches like Marxism and Freudian studies because it attempts to understand how the Western literary imagination functions in structures that originated in the Bible, the "great code" of Western civilization. Marxist and Freudian approaches, on the other hand, import economic-historical and psychological models, respectively, with which to analyze a text. By trying to understand how the narrative of the Bible has influenced other poets' creation of narrative and examining how patterns of imagery and metaphor build a structure for the creative imagination, I seek to stay within the field of poetic imagination, which has little to do with economics or psychology, but has everything to do with language.

Moreover, I will concede that my typological analysis ultimately fails to find "The" meaning in Shakespeare's *Henriad*. Discovering that there is a pattern of the Scriptural mosaic that Shakespeare weaves throughout the plays of the *Henriad* that does follow a Biblical narrative model is significant. My approach does bring the subjective reader of the work or observer of the performance closer to a coherent understanding of the meaning and significance of these plays. It cannot, and should not, however, dethrone the preeminent position of the linguistic transaction that takes place amongst the work or performance, the subjective individual, and the transcendental ideas that the reading or dramatic performance recreates in the creative imagination.

Realizing that this linguistic transaction is the "stuff" of which art is made, I was ultimately led to consider a theory of language in order to better understand how art operates. In the last section of this paper I use the literary essays of a contemporary novelist, Walker Percy, to explore the function of linguistics in the poetic imagination.  In his treatment of "semiotics," the study of the relation of a sign to its signifier, Percy claims that there is a "triadic" relationship, an irreducible triangle with a subjective person, a word or verbal structure (signifier), and a transcendental idea (signified) at each corner, in any human creative transaction[36].  Speaking, the creation of words, is perhaps the most basic transaction (and perhaps the most complicated to explain) between human beings.

Percy's theories answer many of Northrop Frye's concerns about modern language's conception of meaning.  Percy explains that language and art, cannot be made up of "dyadic" relationships, simple action-reaction interaction between subjects and objects (or as Frye would have called them, "causal" interactions).  Instead, Percy suggests that only in a "triadic" relationship (or as Frye would have said a "typological" relationship between the "type," the "antitype," and the subjective person or community which links the two distinct, but related "events") made up of his triangle can art, language, or drama timelessly transfer meaning from one human being (in the case of Shakespeare, the poet) to another human being (the reader or audience) via a "triadic event" (or as Frye would have said a "verbal world" or "vertical dimension of the cosmos")[37].

In many ways this project is ultimately a vindication of Northrop Frye's "great code" and an indication that a paradigm shift in literary criticism must occur soon or the discipline itself will become so fragmented that it, as a whole, will cease to exist. When this shift takes place, the literary critical community will recognize and accept Northrop Frye's later works as the cornerstone of a structure that a unified literary critical community can build founded upon the axiom that "Criticism can and should make sense of literature"[38].

My development of Frye's "great code," which I have used as a means to clarify the role of the numerous Biblical allusions and references that Shakespeare recreates in the narrative of these plays, has ultimately led me to an even more important understanding of language and how it reveals the nature of art. The pastiche of theories that I have woven together in this paper has taken over a year to understand and develop, and is still in what I consider to be an immature form. It is my hope that this initial research project will eventually lead to the further development of these ideas as a uniform approach to unlocking the influences of both the Bible and language on art, literature, and drama.

I am very grateful to Professors Tim O'Brien and Michael Jasperson for sparking my interest in the Bible and Shakespeare, respectively. It was also Professor Jasperson who hooked me on the second *Henriad*. I am indebted to Professor David Tomlinson and Dr. C.S. Mann who so patiently guided me through my earlier Biblical research project. Without the guidance of Dr. David White, who made me realize the powerful combination of Shakespeare and the Bible, none of this would have been possible.

## PART I - HISTORICAL BACKGROUND

I.   PUTTING SHAKESPEARE INTO CONTEXT

As stated in the introduction, an analysis of Shakespeare's *Henriad* should recognize the importance of placing the poet and the work of literature or drama into context. While the first part of this paper attempts to do this, it does not pretend to be a definitive, all-encompassing study of Shakespeare. This being a literary, not a historical study, the focus of this paper is on ideas, not fact patterns.

Determining the context of the poet is always an enigmatic pseudo-historical process. In the case of Shakespeare, however, it means considering the influences on Shakespeare, the man, by understanding both the world in which he lived and any educational, religious, and dramatic experiences that may have influenced his creation of the *Henriad*. As for placing Shakespeare's dramas into context, this means understanding the dramatic influences on Shakespeare and coming to the realization that his plays come out of a long dramatic tradition.

II.  HISTORICAL SHAKESPEARE

A. THE "TRUE" SHAKESPEARE

Since the printing of the First Folio in 1623, there has been debate over the true authorship and authenticity of Shakespeare's plays[39]. In the mid-eighteenth century Delia Bacon first suggested that "Will the Jester, that illiterate peasant from Warwickshire, did not write the plays that go by his name"[40]. Despite all of the controversy, however, there remains enough physical evidence from the late sixteenth and early seventeenth centuries to chronicle factually "the most crucial events" of Shakespeare's life: birth, marriage, and death[41].

Birth, marriage, and death form perhaps the most fundamental cycle of the human condition, and Shakespeare, though his drama would later prove immortal, certainly experienced all three and proved himself mortal. Yet a record of baptism, a marriage license, and a death certificate tell us little of the only man in history who was able to recreate so fully the drama of the human condition on the stage. The search through thousands of historical records over hundreds of years has yielded only an unimaginable amount of speculation about William Shakespeare. Even the most careful scholarship by the most thorough researchers has produced only a sketchy biography that briefly outlines Shakespeare's comings and goings. It is difficult therefore to point to a definitive biography of the "true" William Shakespeare of Stratford-upon-Avon[42].

What we do know about Shakespeare is that tradition holds that he was born on 23 April, 1564, and the record shows he was baptized three days later[43]. On 28 November, 1582 he was married to Anne Hawthaway in Worcester[44]. Between 1589 and 1613, Shakespeare wrote 37 plays for the London stage. Shakespeare died on 23rd of April, 1616, in Stratford-Upon-Avon on his 52nd birthday[45]. In November of 1623, the First Folio of Shakespeare's works was printed[46].

Despite these facts, however, the plays themselves illustrate the true William Shakespeare. Where historical fact innately lacks the ability to tell the story of a man's life, Shakespeare's plays dramatize the tragedy, the laughter, the struggle, and the victory that are parts of all of our lives. It is only in the realm of the dramatic, therefore, that one can see Shakespeare as he truly was--a man.

To get to the man behind the genius we too often look at piles of dry historical facts and discover only details that we possess certainty, which tell us very little. Rather than simply dwelling on fact, I will, like many who have gone before me, do some speculating. I will not, however, use inductive means to simply extrapolate the life of Shakespeare from the bits of fact that we do possess. A "truer" understanding of Shakespeare can only come from a deductive exploration of Shakespeare's age in order to place him, as a man, in time.

## B. CAUGHT BETWEEN MEDIEVAL AND MODERN WORLDS

Placing Shakespeare as a man in time is an affirmation that he was a product of his age. This is clear from his drama that simultaneously portrays the new Elizabethan world order heavily influenced by scientific thought and the Protestant Reformation, and the old medieval world order defined by the ancient dogma of the Roman Catholic Church. In fact, the major tension in Shakespeare's life would have been over religion.

In 1517, Martin Luther nailed his "Ninety-five Theses" on the door of a Church in Wittenberg, Germany, causing a cataclysmic crack in Christianity on continental Europe. It was not until 1534, however, that England, under the leadership of Henry VIII, passed the "Act of Supremacy" that first denied the authority of the Catholic Church in England[47]. Edward VI upheld his father's newly established religion in England for his short reign between 1547 and 1553. His more mature successor, Mary Tudor, however, reintroduced Catholicism during her reign from 1553-1558. Although "[t]he protestant government of Edward IV and the catholic government of Mary were both the beginnings of a development in definitive directions," they were both "too short to produce a permanent result in either direction"[48].

Until 1558, when Queen Elizabeth ascended the throne, England did not have lasting religious leadership. Elizabeth, however, passing the Supremacy Bill and Uniformity Bill in 1559 [making attendance to the Church of England mandatory], "severed England finally from the Roman church"[49]. Mary, Queen

of Scotland, who was both Catholic and the direct descendant of Henry VII,
posed a direct threat to Elizabeth's throne. She was executed in 1587 as a
"convicted conspirator against Elizabeth's throne"[50]. Unfortunately for England,
however, this sparked Philip II to unleash the Spanish Armada on England in
an attempt to "overthrow" the "English heretics"[51]. Although the Armada
ultimately failed, it most vividly represented the passionate religious turmoil
between Protestants and Catholics during Shakespeare's life.

## C. EDUCATION & RELIGIOUS INFLUENCE

Just as the tension between the old and new religions certainly played a part in the politics of Shakespeare's day, they also were a large factor in his education. The "nature and extent of his religious training during boyhood" consisted mainly of "[t]hree institutions" that "contributed to [his] training: the home, the school, and the church"[52]. The influence of each of these institutions was fragmented however, caught between the new and the old: "the influence of the home was Catholic, of the school both Catholic and Protestant, and of the church, Protestant"[53].

In the home, Shakespeare was undoubtedly influenced by his father, who was a devout Catholic. Even after Elizabeth had passed laws making attendance in Anglican Church services mandatory, John Shakespeare, William's father, refused to attend, becoming a "nonconformist hero of the faith"[54]. Moreover, John Shakespeare in his "will" makes a "declaration of his faith and pious resolution" as a Catholic[55].

In the local "Free-School" Shakespeare received an impressive education by today's standards. He would have learned his A-B-C's, the Catechism, the Book of Common Prayer, the New Testament, Grammar, Latin and some Greek as well as having read Cicero, Cæsar, Virgil, Horace and Ovid[56]. Because of Elizabeth's mandate to integrate new Anglican teaching materials into the schools, almost every religious textbook used was "Protestant in contents and tone"[57]. Yet the possibility of a Catholic instructor and the "Catholic influence of his home" would have tempered the "Protestantizing effects of these textbooks," creating a mixed environment of both Anglican and Catholic learning[58]. There can be no doubt that Elizabeth's mandate that all the churches in England become Anglican was carried out. In Stratford-upon-Avon, young Shakespeare would have been required to attend Church services of "the Rev. Mr. Heycroft," who brought with him the "new spirit" of "Protestantism"[59]. Over Shakespeare's life "the influence of the church would have become more and more Protestant" as well[60].

While the division between the Catholic and Protestant churches certainly factored into Shakespeare's education at home, in school, and in the church, it certainly did not limit his knowledge of the Bible. From an examination of his plays alone it is apparent that "[t]here is hardly a book of the Old or the New Testament which is not represented at least by some chance word or phrase in one or other" of Shakespeare's works[61]. And it is in the plays that the religion tensions in Shakespeare's life are "[t]ransmuted into art" giving "depth, fullness, and meaning to the conflicting despairs and aspirations of universal man"[62].

## D. DRAMATIC INFLUENCE

Beyond the political world of Shakespeare's day and the educational

influences on him, Shakespeare wrote his plays from a rich religious-dramatic

heritage. In the fourteenth century, "the existence of liturgical plays in a

number of ecclesiastical centers" merged with "the Feast of Corpus Christi" to

form what are now called the "English Mystery plays" that were performed to

celebrate "the completion of the sacrifice of Christ"[63]. What eventually

developed was a series of "pageants" that presented "the story of Christ from

Adam to Eve to Judgement Day"[64].

These plays were performed in a cycle by different guilds who would

present their piece of the story on a "moveable platform which served as a

stage," called a *"pageant*," the term "originally applied" to the moveable platform

itself, but soon was transformed "from the framework to the play exhibited upon

it"[65]. These plays would take place annually on "Trinity Sunday" with every

guild becoming "responsible for the presentation of a single pageant, or scene,

furnishing its own moveable stage, and meeting all the expenses of the pageant

from its own treasury"[66]. The performance of the mystery plays took place

mainly in the large towns of York, Chester, and Coventry[67]. These plays

continued from the fourteenth century until the "last recorded performance of a

complete cycle...at Coventry in 1580"[68].

While there is no way to know, it is quite possible that "Shakespeare as

a youth of fifteen might conceivably have seen one of the last performances of the guild plays at nearby C ventry"[69]. Whether or not Shakespeare saw a cycle of these plays, however, "[t]he Mysteries left their traces on Shakespeare's art"[70]. In the First *Henriad* "the epic transformation of Shakespeare's amorphous chronicle sources found its only precedent in the Mystery plays"[71]. The parallels of Shakespeare's second *Henriad* to the Mystery plays exists as well, with *Richard II* using a direct reference to "the play of the Agony and the Betrayal in the medieval York cycle of Mystery Plays"[72].

This brief historical sketch of Shakespeare and his time suggests that the religious conflict between the old Catholic and the new Protestant infused his world. What is even more clear, however, is that the Bible and religion permeated every aspect of his life, from his education to the dramatic influences on him. It is apparent that Shakespeare, "[l]ike certain characters of his coming into their happiness...appeared when the time was 'mellow' or ripe" for his creative imagination to harness both the religious tension and Biblical understanding of his time[73]. Paradoxically, only the intersection of the old and the new could create "[t]his ripened time" that "is the Shakespearian moment"[74].

## PART II - CRITICAL APPROACH

I.   THE "GREAT CODE"

A. THE "GREAT CODE" IN THE BIBLE: TYPOLOGY

The discussion of Northrop Frye's "'great code' principle" in the

introduction of this paper suggests that a reading of the Bible offers a means of

understanding Western literature because the "organizing structures of the Bible

and the corresponding structures of 'secular literature' reflect each other"[75]. The

"great code" to which Frye refers is a complex structure of myth and metaphor

that operates throughout the Bible via typology, which is itself a mode of

metaphor. Before examining the question of how myth and metaphor link the

Bible to Western literature or the question of how a typological approach to the

Bible can also be valid for Western literature, it is of primary importance to

establish what typology is and how it operates.

Typological interpretation, which began with St. Paul and St. Augustine,

became the focus of the Christian search for meaning in the Bible. Because

the Bible was viewed as a document complete unto itself that could not be

verified by outside sources, however, this search led to an understanding of the

Bible through the relationships between the Old and New Testaments, which

"form a double mirror, each reflecting the other, but neither the world outside"[76].

A system of interpreting the Bible was eventually developed that looked for

ways in which the New Testament was "concealed" in the Old Testament, and

Old Testament was "revealed" in the New Testament[77].

Typology interprets "certain historical events, persons, and things in the Old Testament" as "precursors ('types') of corresponding elements" in the New Testament, particularly "in the life of Christ and in the Christian life of believers"[78]. "The New Testament," then becomes, among other things, "the key to the Old Testament," by providing "an explanation of what the Old Testament really means"[79]. An event in the Old Testament becomes a "'type' or adumbration of something that happens in the New Testament"[80]. The event in the New Testament is called an "antitype" because it complements the Old Testament "type," becoming "a realized form, of something foreshadowed in the Old Testament"[81].

The most important aspect of the type-antitype pair is not that an antitype is a "realized form" of a type, but that the juxtaposition of type with antitype has a greater meaning than either type or antitype in particular. In general, types tend to look forward, foreshadowing New Testament events, promising the fulfillment of the Old Testament covenant, and making prophecies about the future. Antitypes, on the other hand, look to the past to reveal prefigured understanding, to preserve the promises of the covenant, and to fulfill past prophecy. Types and antitypes, therefore, are two pieces of a puzzle, each with its own meaning and significance, that when fitted together reveal the greater meaning of the puzzle itself.

Typology is the most common method of finding meaning in Biblical narrative. An example of a basic Christian typological relationship in the Bible is the connection of the passover in the book of Exodus to the passion of Christ in the New Testament. For the people of Israel in the Old Testament, the sacrifice of a lamb "without blemish" (Exodus 12:5) meant salvation from God's final plague on the Pharaoh that would kill "every firstborn in the land of Egypt" (Exodus 11:5). The passover is important in and of itself because it retells the history of the people of Israel in exiled Egypt. It is also, however, a key to understanding Christ's passion in the New Testament. The passover acts as a type to which Christ's passion on the cross becomes the antitype. Christ, at the moment of crucifixion, became the sacrificial lamb for all mankind. The greater meaning of the juxtaposition of these two events is that the sacrifice of the blood and flesh of the one can allow for the salvation of the many.

Typological understanding was first located in the New Testament of the Bible. Northrop Frye cites Paul's description "of Adam as a *typos* of Christ," (Romans 5:14) and Peter's counter-description of "Christian baptism as the *antitypos* of the story of the flood" (I Peter 3:21) as the foundation of typology[82]. These examples, however, being only two of the many that occur "explicitly in the New Testament itself," indicate that typology is the "right" way of understanding the Bible critically ("right in the only sense that criticism can recognize, as the way that conforms to the intentionality of the book itself and to the conventions it assumes and requires")[83].

## B. THE "GREAT CODE" IN WESTERN LITERATURE: TYPOLOGY?

Typology may be the "right" method from which to extract meaning from the Bible, but is it also a generally valid means of gaining an understanding of Western literature, particularly Shakespeare's history plays? In order to evaluate this question one must first go back to the role of metaphor, through which typology works, in both the Bible and Western literature.

Northrop Frye argues in *The Great Code: The Bible and Literature* that "much of the Bible" is written in "a metaphorical phase of language, where many aspects of verbal meaning cannot be conveyed except through metaphorical and poetic means"[84]. Frye goes on to say that "myth and metaphor form the primary language" of the Bible; and that because of the Bible's centrality to the Western, Judeo-Christian heritage, the verbal structures that create myth and metaphor in the Bible have influenced Western literature[85]. Frye asserts that this metaphorical and mythological mode of "thinking cannot be superseded, because it forms the framework and context for all thinking," through its use of basic verbal structures. He argues that narrative forms have "descended historically from poetic and mythological ones" to be recreated into the more complex "major verbal structures" used by literature[86]. These metaphorical and mythological structures, which "every human society possesses," are then "transmitted and diversified by literature"[87]. Metaphor and mythology are necessarily, therefore, the link, or "common language," between "Western literature and the Bible"[88].

Despite the fact that the Bible is actually composed of a "small library" of "little books" that appears to be a "confused and inconsistent jumble" of stories, poetry, history, and religious doctrine, Frye reasons that the Bible "has traditionally been read as a unity" and therefore "has influenced Western imagination as a unity"[89]. While the narrative structures of the Bible have not necessarily been directly or intentionally mimicked or copied by Western literature, they have permeated the Western imagination through the Judeo-Christian religious tradition. The Bible has been used for centuries in Western civilization as the most basic educational instrument. All members of medieval society, from the lowest peasant to the king, knew the narratives and religious images from the stories in the Bible; these images formed the core of Western imaginative understanding from which art was created. The earliest forms of English drama, the mystery plays, illustrate the manifestation of this Biblical understanding in art; moreover, the presentation of these plays in a pattern that proceeded from the fall of Adam to the passion of Christ reinforces the typological narrative understanding of the Bible.

Certainly the influence of these traditions on the Western imagination has dwindled since the development of scientific empiricism (c. 1600-1700) and the industrial revolution (c. 1750-1850), which shifted the focus of Western thought away from religion (and therefore the Bible) to that of science. The effect of the Bible on the Western imagination has had a lasting impact, however, creating "an imaginative framework--a mythological universe...--within which Western literature had operated down to the eighteenth century and to a large extent is still operating"[90]. While this paper is not interested in pinpointing an exact date when the continuity of the Biblical traditions of Western civilization broke down, it is important to recognize that the total fragmentation of this tradition occurred sometime after Shakespeare's death in 1616. Shakespeare, living from 1564 to 1616, would have been immersed in this Biblical tradition from the day of his birth until the day of his death. Even if Shakespeare had wanted to avoid his Western heritage, Northrop Frye points out that while "[w]e are free, up to a point, to shape our beliefs," we "are clearly not free...to alter what is really part of our cultural genetic code"[91].

The "great code" of metaphor and mythology may operate in both the Bible and Western literature, but it is obviously more difficult to utilize a typological approach to literary works outside the Bible, because most do not possess the symmetrical "double mirror" form of the Bible, nor are most directly or intentionally concerned with Biblical ideas and images. The primary factor in the complicated equation to evaluate whether a work can be examined typologically, however, remains the creative imagination. The Bible "proceeds from the beginning to the end of its story" with a "sequence or dialectical progression of narrative"[92]. The creative imagination controls the creation of this narrative progression (or, method of story telling). If the author's creative imagination has been influenced by the Judeo-Christian heritage of Western civilization, typology is probably an appropriate critical approach because the narrative structures of the work of literature have been influenced, either directly or indirectly, by the "mythological framework" of the Bible[93]. This is a controversial point amongst literary critics.

Frye argues, however, that the "great code" of myth and metaphor from which typological understanding has been developed is in effect the "cultural genetic code" of Judeo-Christian heritage[94]. Frye describes the "cultural aura...that insulates [man] from nature" as consisting of metaphorical mythology, "or the total structure of human creation conveyed by words, with literature at its center"[95]. This metaphorical mythology, like the Bible, "belongs to the mirror, not the window," and is "designed to draw a circumference around human society and reflect its concerns" back to man, "not to look directly at the nature outside"[96].

Because mythology, which is at the root of the creative imagination, is reflective, not transparent, man is innately subjective. He, in effect, sees the world through himself. Metaphor and mythology then become, as Frye says, "the embryo of literature and the arts," attempting to understand man's spiritual condition in the world[97]. Frye claims that science, the exploration of man's physical condition in the world, is excluded from mythological or metaphorical understanding, however, because scientist can never make "direct [objective] statements about nature" from his inherently subjective vantage[98]. "No form of art," according to Frye, "has anything to do with making direct statements about nature, mistaken or correct"[99]. Conversely, science subtly attacks the entire premise of art by assuming objectivity can be achieved. [Is there any wonder why the mythological framework created by the Bible is shattered after the introduction of scientific empiricism and the industrial revolution?] Frye holds that science can never "replace mythology" or metaphor as the center of human understanding because science attempts to look objectively at nature, not realizing that "man does not live directly and nakedly in nature like animals, but within an envelope that he has constructed out of nature, the envelope usually called culture or civilization"[100]. Moreover, this envelope is created at its most fundamental level out of verbal structures that have a common or "true" meaning to the entire culture.

Frye makes the same distinction between "fact" and "truth" discussed earlier in this paper. Art approaches "truth" when it downplays "fact" through metaphor to create a transcendental reality of ideas. Frye claims that "[o]ur cultural heritage" comes from a common, subjective, "social past," not the apparently objective past documented as factual, "historical record," and that it is "a gross error in perspective either to detach the cultural from the historic past or to confuse the two" because all meaning will be lost without the relationships holding them together[101]. Only from a subjective vantage, therefore, can man understand and find meaning in "the great dreams of the arts, which keep recurring to haunt us with a sense of how little we know of the real dimensions of our own experience"[102].

Likewise, Frye asserts that any meaning found "within the Bible itself, all the values connected with the term 'truth,'" can be reached only by passing through myth and metaphor"[103]. Just as typology can be used to isolate and examine meaning in the Bible, therefore, it can also be used to examine works of art forged from the Judeo-Christian creative imagination that is flooded with this Biblical, mythological understanding. The mirror that reflects images in the Old Testament to the New Testament is the same mirror that the artist uses to understand the human condition. The typological event in the Bible is a typological motif in literature "that has to be repeated in different context throughout" the Bible or the work of literature for meaning to be conveyed[104]. Intuitively, this makes sense of Northrop Frye's statement that: "Page one of the Bible says that God created the world; page one of the critic's handbook, not yet written, tells him that what he is studying are human creations"[105].

## C. THE NATURE OF HISTORY: TYPOLOGY & CAUSALITY

A paper concerning the Bible and Shakespeare's history plays must inevitably ask the question: What is the nature of History? The modern historian's answer would invariably involve an objective, scientific approach to understanding the past through examination of historical facts and artifacts. To the writers of the Bible and to Shakespeare, however, this approach would seem somewhat lopsided because it ignores the historian's own subjective understanding of the past and his knowledge of his contemporary audience. The first step in answering this question, therefore, is to realize that the notion of what history is has changed significantly in our modern age.

The writers of the Bible were not historians, nor did they ascribe their methods of recording history to the scientific approach that modern historians use. Although "[B]iblical writers...often expressed themselves in the historical mode," presenting "their religious message in the form of narratives about events and people," the Bible itself "cannot be properly read as a history book"[106]. The same is true of Shakespeare's history plays which are also written in a historical mode, but also have a greater purpose than simply chronicling the past. In order to extricate Biblical or Shakespearian meaning that is tangled up in historical narrative, the reader must be "aware of the importance of all the standard figures of speech" employed in the Bible and Shakespeare, and the "most important" being metaphor[107].

Metaphor is the medium through which meaning is transmitted in both the Bible and Shakespeare. Unfortunately, many people read and interpret the Bible literally, as if its only function were to chronicle the facts of Biblical history. To illustrate what an outrageous approach this really is, consider someone who interpreted Shakespeare's history plays by assuming that their primary purpose was to record English history. Metaphor does not function literately, imposing a "this is this," or an "I mean what I say" relationship. Instead, metaphor juxtaposes "two points of verbal reference" creating a "this means that" relationship that is inherently more complicated than the literal approach[108]. The metaphorical relationship must exist in time, however, and is therefore dependent on "two figures of speech that exist in time" to relay its meaning: typology and causality[109]. Typology conveys meaning in a way that would seem familiar and natural to both the writers of the Bible and to Shakespeare. Causality, on the other hand, attempts to understand relationships in the way a modern historian would.

Typology, as a mode of metaphor, looks forward in time to assign meaning, from the type that has occurred to the antitype that will fulfill, or bring new meaning or form to the type. Typology, therefore, as Frye describes it, "relates to the future" and is associated with "faith, hope, and vision"--the fulfillment of the covenant, and the revelation of the prophecy--and ultimately with "truth"[110]. What typology "both assumes and leads to," however, "is a theory of history or more accurately of historical process: an assumption that there is some meaning or point" to events that occur in life[111]. While typology is concerned with meaning, however, it allows the type and the antitype to create a greater metaphorical understanding to convey that meaning. This approach to understanding history does not attempt to delineate cause and effect, but rather attempts to narrate a story which has metaphorical meaning understood in a typological context. This narrative approach to history would have been how both Shakespeare and the authors of the Bible understood the stories which they recreated.

A historical process that finds meaning through assigning causes to events, that is much closer to the modern notion of history, is known as causality. Causality is a mode of metaphor like typology that "moves in time;" however, it moves "in the opposite direction" from typology[112]. In typology, the "type exists in the past and the antitype in the present, or the type exists in the present and the antitype in the future"[113]. The occurrence of the event in the present or the promise of the event in the future will clarify the meaning of the past type, and through their juxtaposition in time become an "antitype of what has happened previously"[114]. There is no concern with knowing why the antitype has occurred, only in establishing a greater metaphorical "truth" from the juxtaposition of type and antitype. Causality, on the other hand, as Frye describes it, reverses the "temporal order of typology," understanding events by "thinking of them as effects" and searching "for their prior causes"[115]. These causes become "the antitypes of their effects" or "revelations of the real meaning of the existence of their effects"[116].

Based on "reason, observation, and knowledge," causality looks to the past for meaning because the past is "all that we genuinely or systematically know"[117]. Confronted by "a mass of phenomena" of "events" the causal thinker "can understand only by thinking of them as effects, after which he searches for their prior causes"[118]. Once meaning has been assigned to an effect, or antitype, by reaching back to a causal type, a reversal in the thought process occurs that explains the "movement from cause to effect" as if it naturally occurred this way[119]. This reversal occurs in order to create a greater sense of "clarity," the logical process of thinking proceeding "forward from cause to effect"[120]. Frye points out that the most common form of "verbal expression" for causality, is, of course, "continuous prose, which seems to have been developed mainly for the purpose of putting causality into verbal structures"[121]. The "simple prose statement," for example, "The man opened the door," illustrates "the link between the subject-predicate-object arrangement of prose" that gives the illusion that an event has logically proceeded "from cause to effect"[122]. Temporally experienced, however, the door is opened and then the man comes through it.

Because causality appears to move logically from cause to effect, it gives the illusion that it is like typology moving from type to antitype. The rhetorical structure of both causality and typology are so similar in form that "typology might in fact be thought of as an analogy of causality"[123]. Frye indicates, however, that the distinguishing factor between causality and typology is that "[c]ausal thinking tends not to move out of the same dimension of time...the causes have to be in the same temporal plane as their effects or they are not genuine causes," while "[t]ypology points to future events that are often thought of as transcending time, so they contain a vertical lift as well as a horizontal move forward"[124]. It is this "vertical lift" that Frye describes that allows the type in typology to transcend temporal reality to coexist with the antitype and create a greater metaphorical meaning than either a type or an antitype alone. The argument that causality and typology are similar based on the fact that "types are frequently established, or at least interpreted as such, only after the antitypes have appeared," still cannot account for the "vertical lift" that takes place in typology which allows the type-antitype pair to assume a new and greater metaphorical understanding[125].

The modern approach to history is causal and attempts to examine the past to ascribe meaning to that which has occurred. To the modern historian, the future is unknowable, unpredictable, and therefore only understandable after it has occurred. Like causality, the modern notion of History relies on "reason, observation, and knowledge," again seeking only that which we can "genuinely or systematically know," and mimicking science in its attempt to get at "fact"[126]. Modern history, as opposed to typological historical narrative, therefore, attempts fundamentally to be a scientific procedure because causality is the "essential basis" or mode of "scientific" thinking[127]. Modern history, therefore, misses the greater "truth" that historical narrative can illustrate through typological relationships. Typology understands events not as historical "facts" that move from cause to effects, but rather as metaphorical moments that create a greater understanding of meaning when paired together in type-antitype form.

History that is related through narrative, however, is linked not to science, but to religion. Religion, like historical narrative, operates typologically, looking to the future for the predictable and inevitable fulfillment of God's promise. Modern history, however, ironically relies on faith, which Frye indicates is "the legacy of Biblical typology," in that "our belief [is] that despite apparent confusion, even chaos, in human events...those events are going somewhere and indicating something"[128]. It is ironic that the notion of modern history relies on typological faith because both typology and religion are "clearly not, like causality [and modern history], anything that can be linked to a scientific or philosophical procedure," belonging instead to the realm of "hope" and "vision"[129].

The difference between typological narrative history and modern causal history is similar to the dichotomy between religion and science or "truth" and "fact." Historical narrative in fact "grows quite naturally out of theology and is never separated from it"[130]. It follows, therefore that an understanding of historical narrative and religion should also be linked.

Religion, or more specifically, religious meaning found in the Bible, can also be revealed through typology[131]. If the jump from the Bible to religion seems inappropriate, consider the fact "the doctrines of Christian theology" form "the antitypes of which the stories and maxims in the Bible, including those in the New Testament, are types"[132]. An example would be the taking of the Eucharist, which is the antitype of Christ's passion. Christ's death only has meaning to the Christian after partaking of the bread and wine that is the body and blood of Christ. At this moment, time experiences a "vertical lift as well as a horizontal move forward" and Christ's crucifixion transcends time[133]. These two events are now linked by the movement in time from the "type" to the "antitype" and through the vertical lift that transcends temporal reality.

Typology, however, is not just a "Christian view of the Bible," as some critics argue[134]. Although "Christian interpretation" does use typology as a means to explain that "everything that happens in the Old Testament is a 'type' or 'figure' of which the New Testament provides the 'antitype' or revealed meaning," typology "is not confined to the Christian perspective"[135]. Typology applies to the "Jewish point of view," just as logically as the Christian "without the New Testament as with it, and its antitypes are still the restoration of Israel and the coming of the Messiah, though the context of these events is different from that of Christianity" [136]. The point being that typology can be applied to literature without necessitating a Christian interpretation.

Typology is also not just a means of religiously understanding the Bible. The reason Shakespeare's history plays so naturally lend themselves to typological interpretation is that they have their roots in historical narrative, which is typological in nature. The reason that typology is also valid as a tool for interpretation of other works of literature is that literary narrative, like historical narrative, tells its story through the literary device of plot. A story with a plot is establishing, on at least one level, a factual or fictional narrative that creates its own history becoming a meta-historical narrative. From this meta-historical narrative, typology can find meaning through examining images and verbal structures that occur in motifs.

Frye holds that this is not an allegorical understanding of a narrative passage even though typology does have "affinities with allegory" in that "the stories or myths of the Old Testament [and New Testament] become types or parables of existential truths" that make up allegory[137]. The "normal structure of allegory," however, dwells in the realm of "an imaginary narrative paralleled with the moral precepts which are its 'real meaning,'"[138]. Neither the Bible nor any work, particularly a history play, that reveals its story through the development of characters and plot, is concerned with an "imaginary narrative," but rather with "people and events"[139].

The Bible, in particular, "where both Testaments are concerned with actual people and events," does not fit the allegorical model precisely because of its typological basis[140]. Typology, with its connection to religion, becomes a "vision of history," or a narrative historical "process," that must be connected to "actual events and people" in the Bible[141]. Frye indicates that it is "the typology of the Bible," which necessitates the important role of historical antecedents or types, that "links it to history in a way impossible for paganism, which remains based on the recurring cycles of nature"[142]. Historical narrative in the Bible therefore is "diachronic," having a "distinctive sense of history" that flows from its "typological structure"[143].

The "diachronic dimension" of historical narrative "makes it possible for personality to emerge in Biblical mythology"[144]. The distinguishing factor that separates literature that has been influenced by the Bible and most other literary traditions is, therefore, that the Bible possesses a diachronic nature which recognizes both the importance of historical antecedents or types, and that "it is only within this historical context that personality can emerge"[145]. Frye holds that most literature influenced by religions outside the Judeo-Christian tradition, however, creates a "synchronic mythology," meaning that historical antecedents are ignored in favor of allegorical symbolism[146].

The essence of personality makes the Bible unique from other religious heritages. Frye concludes that while "Jesus and Adonis are both 'dying gods,' in the sense of being objects of cults with similar imagery and ritual attached to them," Jesus ultimately is a historical person and Adonis is only a mythological figure, regardless of "however many human figures may have represented him"[147]. While both figures may symbolize suffering, the diachronic sense of typological, historical narrative in the Bible gives Christ's death an even more significant meaning in that the passion was preceded by the passover, and is commemorated through the taking of the Eucharist. The synchronic nature of

Adonis, on the other hand, traps his figure in only one moment of time, isolated without historical antecedent or typological antitype.

It is precisely this diachronic nature of the Bible that makes a typological interpretation of Shakespeare's history plays attractive. Just as Biblical narrative deals with "actual events and people," so do Shakespeare's history plays[148]. Moreover, the development of characters in Shakespeare's dramas parallels the important role of personality in the diachronic nature of Biblical, historical narrative. Shakespeare, having been immersed in the Judeo-Christian Heritage of the West, certainly understood the importance of character in telling narrative history. While modern historical method might point to the factual employment of the long-bow by the English at the battle of Agincourt in 1415 as the decisive factor in the English victory, Shakespeare understood and exemplified in his historical narrative that the leadership and character of Henry V was truly the decisive element to the English victory.

What finally links Shakespeare's history plays with the Bible is that both Shakespeare and the authors of the Bible employ the same sense of historical narrative. Just as typology is a valid means of analyzing Biblical, historical narrative, so too is it a valid means of approaching Shakespearian, historical narrative because both sources understand the truth of history in the same way, through metaphor. While modern historians would look for a causal understanding of the facts of the past in order to record history, Shakespeare and the writers of the Bible "told their stories of the past...not for the sake of the past, but for the sake of the present--their present[149]. There was no concern among the authors of the Bible nor Shakespeare to relate their narratives of history accurately, instead "they selected material concerning the past and shaped it according to what they felt were the needs of their own present-day audience"[150]. This was not a matter of lying or being factually inconsistent, but rather a concern with telling the truth of the past in a way that would carry more meaning to the present.

Many literary critics regard Northrop Frye's *The Great Code* as "anti-historical because it seemed a priori unlikely on historical grounds that the unity of narrative and imagery it demonstrated could exist in the Bible"[151]. Frye's arguments for understanding the Bible and Western literature are insightful, however, precisely because they see beyond the modern objective approach to history and realize instead that historical narrative does operate through unified patterns of imagery and structure. While agreement with this point is unlikely, Frye is content to state that as this unity "does exist, so much the worse for history, but not everyone is prepared yet for such a paradigm shift" because "there are still far too many literary critics who are both ignorant and contemptuous of the mental processes that produce literature"[152].

## II. THE "GREAT CODE" IN SHAKESPEARE'S *HENRIAD*

### A. NORTHROP FRYE'S TYPOLOGICAL "PHASES"

Beyond the typological approach to understanding Biblical narrative discussed above, Northrop Frye also delineates in *The Great Code* "seven main [typological] phases" that he asserts are always found in Biblical narrative[153]. Frye describes the sequence of these phases as a "dialectical progression" of what he refers to as the "revelation" of the content and meaning of the Bible[154]. What Frye is actually alluding to is the "revelation" of Biblical, historical narrative that "proceeds from the beginning to end of its story" in a sequential pattern of typology[155]. The sequence of these phases moves from creation through revolution (or exodus), law, wisdom, prophecy, gospel, and finally to apocalypse[156]. The first five of these phases "have their center of gravity in the Old Testament," while the last two focus on the New Testament[157].

Frye claims that each phase acts as "a type of the one following it and an antitype of the one preceding it"[158]. This means that creation is a type to which revolution is the antitype; at the same time creation is also an antitype for which apocalypse is its type. Frye in his description of each phase indicates typical imagery and events that occur in each phase of the typological cycle of Biblical narrative. From Frye's discussion of these images and events, it becomes apparent that there are two additional sub-phases occurring in the cycle. Between the phases of creation and revolution there must necessarily be a phase including the fall of man, that has disturbed the "perfect world" of

God's creation and thrown man into a phase of revolution[159]. Also, between the phases of prophecy and gospel, there occurs a movement toward the "eventual restoration" of man to "an original state of...happiness" that is indicated by a phase including "the Incarnation or the Resurrection" of God on earth[160]. The final cycle then with the two additional sub-phases has nine elements that act alternately as type and antitype to each another, proceeding from creation, through fall, revolution (or exodus), law, wisdom, prophecy, incarnation (or resurrection), gospel, and apocalypse. A simple model of this progression is seen in figure 1 on the next page. According to Frye, each of these phases is characterized by certain typological events and images that connect the phases together in type-antitype pairs. The major imagery and events of these nine typological phases are discussed below. Each phase is a type which leads to the next phase as an antitype. The overall effect of all nine phases is the "revelation" of the meaning of the Scriptures through the retelling, or narration, of man's story on this world and in the next[161].

Frye indicates that the creation phase of Biblical typology typically includes a verbal creation by a "sky-father" in which "the forms of life are *spoken* into existence, so that while they are made or created, they are not made out of something else"[162]. This masculine creation from nothing, contrasts with pagan "sexual creation myths" in which case life is brought into being cyclically from an "earth-mother"[163]. The creation from an "absolute beginning," necessarily "implies an absolute end," but not the end of life, rather

Figure 1: Frye's Typological Phase Model

NORTHROP FRYE'S TYPOLOGICAL
PHASE MODEL

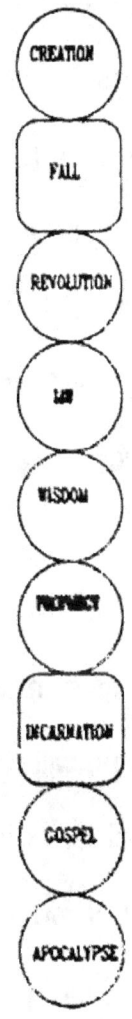

"the end of death"[164]. The creation, therefore, is the antitype to which the apocalypse, the absolute end of time and death, is the type[155].

Frye argues that the male Christian God, being "good," could not have created a world with "any death or sin or misery in it;" therefore his creation is the "model world"[166]. The imagery of this perfect world is typically that of the garden, which "is the symbol of the female body in the Bible"[167]. The tension between the male God who first creates a male human being, Adam, in the mother garden of Eden, and then creates a female human being, Eve, suggests that "man is to leave his parents and become united with his wife" in a holy marriage[163]. After this marriage, man must break from the mother "in order to get born," which is simultaneously a break from the "embryonic life in Mother Nature, enclosed in the mechanical cycle of repetition,...with no freedom to escape"[169].

The fall is the antitype to which the creation is the type. The seeds of the fall, therefore, are found in the seeds of marriage and the propagation of man. Man must choose, of his own free, will (there is no choice in the inevitable cycle of Mother Nature), whether or not to obey his creator-father. Man "lost touch with the divine creation through his own sin," which usually has to do with the quest for knowledge of "good and evil"[170]. This knowledge is usually associated with mortal sex, in which "there is no complete union of bodies" as there should be if man and wife are of "one flesh" as God intended. With knowledge of mortal sex, man first becomes, as Frye explains, "self-conscious, as is sexual knowledge itself," and then becomes "a subject confronting an objective environment"[171].

The fall, therefore, as Frye indicates, is "an alienation myth which expresses the human condition" in a less than perfect world, accounting for "the contrast between the model world that...[a perfect] God must have made and the actual world that we find ourselves in now"[172]. With his newly acquired sense of consciousness, man becomes aware of his death, which is also closely associated with sex, and therefore his mortality. The symbol of the "serpent, with its ability to renew its vitality by shedding its skin," represents the "cyclical world of objective nature man has entered with his fall"[173]. Death therefore, "the most natural of all events, the one thing that we know will always happen, is nevertheless wrong and unnatural, not a part of the original scheme of things"[174].

The imagery most associated with the fall, therefore, is blood, because it is the "life" of man[175]. When blood is spilled, as in birth, it signals the of fall man. Moreover, when the blood is spilled through violence, it is an indication that man has broken from his creator-father, and is severing the life line of humanity that God has created. Frye reasons that to raise man "from his fallen level to his originally designed one involves some degree of returning to his original creation," which is usually a long and fierce "trial" in the fallen world which will eventually end in "judgment"[176].

The starting point of this "trial" in the objective, natural world that man has fallen into, is revolution, which is the antitype to the fall. The typological phase of revolution attempts, according to Frye, to "divide the world" into groups who are "with us" or "against us," in an attempt to establish social order[177]. The movement of revolution, therefore, recognizes that "those with right beliefs or attitudes" will "emerge on top" after their "now powerful enemies [are] rendered impotent"[178].

In the phase of revolution "metaphors of the ear as compared to those of the eye" are important because they signal the beginning and the end of this phase[179]. Revolution begins through "the word listened to and acted upon," which becomes "the starting point of a course of action"[180]. A "visible object" that is an image or sign from God, on the other hand, brings revolution "to a respectful halt in front of it"[181]. The most common image is that of the sun, being associated with the "world ruler," and being the "starting point of the visible world"[182].

While revolution attempts to divide the world into two camps, law delineates what brings a people together. Frye suggests that the type of revolution, seeking to divide, is followed by a unifying "sense of purity in a people linked together by common acts and beliefs"[183]. Through the "shared crisis" of revolution, a community gains a "sense of involvement with its own laws, customs, and institutions" that unifies them with a "sense of being a people set apart"[184].

Law represents both the individual's "obligations to society" and "the tendency in nature to recover its balance after an act of human aggression"[185]. "Law is general," however, applying to all members in a society and demanding that justice be done. The breaking of the law by the individual, therefore, will necessarily be punished by the society in order to reassert the preeminence of the law over the individual.

Frye argues that wisdom, being the antitype of law, "starts with the individualization of law, the individual allowing the law, in its human and moral aspect, to permeate and inform all one's personal life"[186]. The "wise man" in a community then "is the one who follows in the accepted way,...experience and tradition" having shown him the "right way"[187]. The past gives one the "sense of continuity, or persistence" that one can use "as a balancing pole for walking the tightrope of life"[188].

Education, "the attaining of the right forms of behavior and the persistence of them," links wisdom to the past. Wisdom "facing the future," however, is "prudence"[189]. For the wise man, the "human situation" is, as frye describes it, "a kind of horizontal line, formed by precedent and tradition and extended by prudence"[190]. One of the most important expressions of wisdom through tradition is ceremony, which is necessarily linked to the past, but also guarantees order in the future if it is followed with humility. The "present moment" for the wise man, therefore, is one in which "the uncertainties of the future" are "minimized by the observance of the law" that is linked to the past through ceremony[191].

Wisdom is the type for which prophecy is the antitype because "prophecy is geared to the future" in the same way as "wisdom is to the past"[192]. Frye holds that prophecy can look beyond the present moment and see "a comprehensive view of the human situation, surveying it from creation to final deliverance" in the same way that wisdom attempts to see the past through ceremony[193]. While the wise man is trapped into viewing life as a "horizontal line," however, the prophet can see "man in a state of alienation caused by his own distractions, at the bottom of a U-shaped curve"[194]. Frye says that the prophet sees the "present moment" as "an alienated prodigal son, a moment that has broken away from the past but may return to that identity in the future"[195]. The prophet has the vantage point, therefore, to see that the salvation of man and the restoration of the garden is still possible.

The incarnation is the antitype of prophecy because the prophetic vision cannot come true unless God intervenes in human history. Marking the transition between the Old Testament and New Testament typological phases, Frye indicates that the incarnation is the realization that God descended "from the higher level or 'heaven,'" not bounded by time, to the earth and that he will ascend "back to it again" once he has completed his mission on earth[196]. Incarnation seems enigmatic because it always "seems to have taken place historically at one of those dialectical confrontations in which history suddenly expands to myth and indicates a dimension beyond the historical[197]. Christ becomes "an incarnation of God in man," entering time to allow the prophetic vision of restoration to become a reality[198].

Gospel, being a "further intensifying of the prophetic vision," works as the antitype for incarnation[199]. While the incarnation is the "Day of the Lord," Gospel furthers the restoration after Christ has been resurrected[200]. Frye suggests that the key to the "mystery" of Christ's "spiritual kingdom" has been passed to the "initiated," to spread the good news[201]. The "initiated" think of achieving "the spiritual kingdom as a way of life" rather than understanding it "merely as a doctrine"[202]. This "way of life" is one of "repentance," involving a "change of outlook or spiritual metamorphosis" which allows for "an enlarged vision of the dimensions of human life"[203]. One undergoes these changes only after he "repents" of "sin"[204].

Frye argues that sin "means nothing outside a religious and individualized context," and, therefore, "is not [necessarily] illegal or antisocial behavior"[205]. Instead, he indicates that sin is simply "a matter of trying to block the activity of God" which "always results is some curtailing of human freedom, whether of oneself or of one's neighbor"[206]. The existence of sin in the fallen world, however, "splits the world into the kingdom of genuine identity, presented by Jesus's 'home,' and a hell, a conception found in the Old Testament only in the form of death or the grave"[207]. Gospel then acts as the type to incarnation by making man "a 'new creature' (II Corinthians 5:17), in which the original and now fallen order of nature becomes a mother bringing to birth a re-creation made through a union of God and man (Romans 8:21)"[208]. Frye says that this "new creation" of man "is the reappearance in human life of the higher or transfigured nature, the innocent world before the fall," which allows for "power of action informed by a vision transcending time and space"[209]. Frye believes that such a vision will "set one free" of literal law (but of course we cannot "get free of the [literal] law by breaking the [literal] law, only more fouled up in it than ever")[210]. The implication of such a vision, however, means that "man has to fight his way out of history and not simply awaken from it" because God's new law leads man toward "atonement," the reunification of God and man in a spiritual world of heaven rather than the physical world of the earth[211]. The final result of gospel is the splitting of "the world of history into a spiritual kingdom and a hell"[212] which takes place in the antitype to the phase of gospel, apocalypse.

Frye indicates that the apocalypse is a kind of "revelation" of God's final plan "in which the people of God are raised into recognition and heathen kingdoms are cast into darkness"[213]. The coming of this final judgment is preceded in "both social and natural orders" by "plagues, wars, [and] famines," and finally leads to "an eventual transformation, for those who persist in the faith, of the world into a new heaven and earth"[214]. The vision of the second coming, however, is hidden from man who has created "what he calls history" that acts as a "screen to conceal the workings of the apocalypse from himself"[215]. The vision of the apocalypse, is "the vision of the total meaning of the Scriptures," which can "break on anyone at anytime," coming "like a thief in the night (Revelation 16:15)"[216].

When the apocalypse comes it will bring "the destruction of the order of nature" of the world as we know it, "the destruction of the way of seeing that order that keeps man confined to the world of time and history as we know them"[217]. Frye suggests that "Scripture is intended to achieve" this destruction"[218]. The "panoramic" vision of the apocalypse appears to man as an "objective" vision; what it really is, however, is "a projection of the subjective 'knowledge of good and evil' acquired at the fall"[219]. The end of this vision of the physical world is the "final 'judgment' where the world disappears into its two unending constituents, a heaven and a hell, into one of which man automatically goes"[220]. This "panoramic apocalypse ends with the restoration of the tree and water of life, the two elements of the original creation," making the phase of apocalypse a type to which the creation is the antitype[221]. After the apocalypse life may begin again with the marriage of heaven and earth, and the re-creation of the paradisal garden.

This Biblical, typological pattern should hold true for any narrative that has been influenced by the Judeo-Christian heritage because, as William Blake says, "[t]he Old and New Testaments are the Great Code of Art"[222]. Northrop Frye extends Blake's assertion, arguing that this "Great Code" is made up of these specific narrative patterns which should manifest themselves in narrative art created by the "Western imagination"[223].

## B. THE ROYAL METAPHOR: KING AND COUNTRY

After examining Shakespeare's *Henriad* for the manifestation of Frye's typological phases, it became apparent that a subtle typological narrative cycle does operate throughout these four plays. This typological cycle occurs particularly in the life of each king in the *Henriad*, going through all nine typological phases during each one's reign as king. The typological cycles of the kings occur, however, "within the larger, continuing process of which each history play presents a part"[224]. This idea led to the more insightful realization that the "real hero of the English [History] play is England"[225]. England, therefore, representing the garden, goes through a fall and eventual restoration that is based on the actions of each king. This larger cycle in the *Henriad*, however, is not a typological one, other than the fact that it contains the twenty-seven phases of the three kings.

This understanding led to the realization that Shakespeare's *Henriad* manifests Northrop Frye's typological phase cycle through the "royal metaphor." The "royal metaphor" indicates that "the function of the king is primarily to represent, for his subjects, the unity of their society in an individual form," creating the "metaphor of society as a single 'body'"[226]. The origin of this concept is both Biblical and typological in nature, having to do with the society of Israel and with the individual Jesus. The "Old Testament is concerned with the society of Israel" and the "New Testament with the individual Jesus;" the society of Israel, then, becomes "the type of which the individual Jesus is the antitype"[227]. Because "in the world of the royal metaphor...society and individual interpenetrate with each other," the actions of the king and the inevitable consequences of those actions must necessarily be felt by the subjects of the king[228]. The vertical movement of England as a garden going through a fall and restoration, is therefore a function of the King's actions.

The creation of England as a garden stems from the unbroken royal connection from William the Conqueror to King Richard II. When Richard violently spills the blood of his uncle, Thomas of Woodstock, the Duke of Gloucester, England falls into a revolution that ends with Henry Bolingbroke usurping the throne. Henry's actions are valid in that Richard has abdicated his responsibility to his subjects and spilled the blood of his uncle; however, they are also illegitimate in that Richard is the rightfully anointed king ordained by God, and only God can punish Richard for his sins. The result is that the people of England suffer as their blood is shed in civil war.

Bolingbroke's tenure as king is one of stagnation. In seizing the throne and suggesting that Richard be killed (which a loyal subject executes), Henry throws his own kingship into a revolution that will reestablish who is the rightful heir to the throne, spilling more English blood on the now tainted English soil. Despite his dreams of a crusade to the Holy Land, Henry IV must reestablish order in his kingdom, hoping that his prodigal son will be worthy of being the next legitimate heir to the throne.

Young Prince Hal throws off his wastrel youth to become the legitimate heir to the throne, and the ideal Christian monarch. He restores England to its original paradisal condition by leading his subjects to France and winning back the ancestral rights to parts of that kingdom. His kingship ends with a holy marriage of France and England becoming once again a perfect garden.

While this non-typological cycle of the royal metaphor posits the fall and restoration of England as a function of the king, it also dictates the direction of movement of the typological phases that the king goes through. The cycle of the royal metaphor, therefore, modulates the twenty-seven phase typological cycle, according to the direction of motion of the cycle of the royal metaphor. Placing each king's reign on a curve, as shown in Figure 2, illustrates the cycle of the royal metaphor. Depending on the state of the king, and therefore the kingdom, the meaning and imagery of each phase in Frye's typological narrative cycle varies as the kings progress down and then back up again the cycle of the royal metaphor. Richard II's reign includes the fall that England experiences. The reign of Henry IV rounds out the fall, putting an end to revolution and reestablishing social order. Henry V restores England to its previous state of creation. The "central royal metaphor" that Shakespeare creates in the Henriad, therefore, is a vision of the English people as "members of one [unified, social] body," that through "terms of unity and integration" is connected with the garden soil of England, and "absorbed" into the individual body of the king[229].

Figure 2: The Cycle of the Royal Metaphor

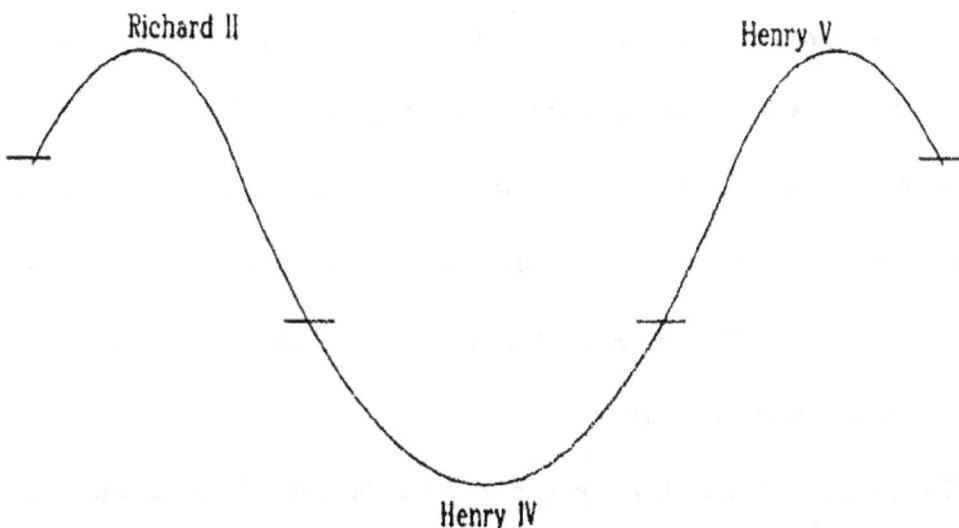

The Garden of England
as seen through
the Royal Metaphor

## C. TYPOLOGICAL, NARRATIVE PHASES IN THE *HENRIAD*

Within Shakespeare's *Henriad*, certain narrative passages correspond with Northrop Frye's typological phases in the royal metaphor as described above. These narrative passages are typological "nodes" that simultaneously look back as an antitype to their type, as well as look forward to their antitype as a type. The basic criteria I used to establish these nodes is as follows: 1) the node would posit an event or image that should occur in its current phase; 2) the node would, as much as possible, look backward to the previous type and forward to the next antitype; 3) because of the royal metaphor, the nodes should either be narrative passages by the king, or narrative passages about the king, or an event in developing the particular phase; 4) the sequence of the nodes in the play should occur chronologically in the plays, but if two phases do not, they should at least be in the same scene; 5) as much as possible, the narrative chosen as a node should be a major speech in the development of the plot or a character in the play.

The phase of typological creation at the beginning of Shakespeare's *Henriad*, in particular the play *Richard II*, has already taken place as the play begins. This creation is not so much a creation of a perfect king, in Richard himself, but rather, the creation of the garden of England, that quite like the garden of Eden is a "model world"[230]. This is the garden that the dying Duke of Lancaster, John of Gaunt, Richard II's noble uncle, describes in his "demi-paradise" narrative at the beginning of Act II, scene i:

This royal throne of kings, this scept'red isle,
This earth of majesty, this seat of Mars,
This other Eden, demi-paradise,
This fortress built by Nature for herself
Against infection and the hand of war,
This happy breed of men, this little world,
This precious stone set in the silver sea
Which serves it in the office of a wall,
Or as a moat defensive to a house,
Against the envy of less happier lands,
This blessed plot, this earth, this realm, this England,
This nurse, this teeming womb of royal kings,
Feared by their breed, and famous by their birth,
Renownèd for their deeds as far from home,
For Christian service and true chivalry,
As is the sepulcher in stubborn Jewry
Of the world's ransom, blessed Mary's son,
This land of such dear souls, this dear land--
Dear for her reputation through the world--
(R2.II.i.40-58)

Gaunt's description of England is actually a past vision of what England once was contrasted with what Richard has made it while he has been king. Further down in the speech, Gaunt refers to Richard's England as "bound in with shame,/ With inky blots, and rotten parchment bonds" referring to Richard's use of blank charters to raise funds for his extravagant tastes and foreign wars (R2.II.i.63-4). The most important images in the narrative, however, describe England as "other Eden" built as a "fortress... Against infection and the hand of war." The royal metaphor begins with the reference to "this happy breed of men, this little world...This nurse, this teeming womb of royal kings," which juxtaposes the line of royal blood with the English people and England herself.

This nodal description of the English garden does occur after the nodes of fall and revolution, so the first node of the first phase is also the greatest

exception to the criteria established above. The reason for this exception is the

clarity of vision that Gaunt's speech has that links it to the next node of the fall.

The main image that links the creation to the fall is that of an established line of

royal blood of which Richard is the most recent king. In Act I, scene ii, the

Duchess of Gloucester indicates clearly why Richard, despite his lineage, has

fallen, becoming a type of Adam. The widow of the murdered Woodstock

condemns Richard in a conversation with Gaunt indicating that this sacred line

of blood has been broken unnaturally by Richard's deed:

> Edward's seven sons, whereof thyself art one,
> Were as seven vials of his sacred blood,
> Or seven fair branches springing from one root.
> Some of those seven are dried by nature's course,
> Some of those branches by Destinies cut;
> But Thomas, my dear lord, my life, my Gloucester,
> One vial full of Edward's sacred blood,
> One flourishing branch of his most royal root,
> Is cracked, and all the precious liquor spilt;
> Is hacked down, and his summer leaves all faded,
> By envy's hand, and murder's bloody ax.
> (R2.I.ii.11-21)

The Duchess of Gloucester's cry of foul play in her husband's death is

much more than expressed anger, focusing on the spilling of the "sacred blood"

of one of Edward III's sons. She creates a tree of life metaphor which

represents the family tree of Edward III. Distinguishing between some

"branches" of the family dying "by nature's course," and her husband who was

"hacked down," Gloucester's widow realizes that there has been a violation of

Edward's tree of life that has brought with it the fall of man in England.

Richard, having caused the fall through the murder of Gloucester, begins

the descent into the phase of revolution that both he and his subjects will face.

Richard's movement downward on the curve of the royal metaphor causes his

typological phase of revolution to be inverted; rather than trying to create social

order from revolution, therefore, Richard has inverted it.

The clearest indications of Richard's inversion of social order have to do

with his reversal of responsibilities to his subjects and of respect, especially as

a king, for his elders, illustrated at the end of Act I:

> We will ourself in person to this war.
> And, for our coffers, with too great a court
> And liberal largess, are grown somewhat light,
> We are enforced to farm our royal realm,
> The revenue whereof shall furnish us
> For our affairs in hand. If that come short,
> Our substitutes at home shall have blank charters,
> Whereto, when they shall know what men are rich,
> They shall subscribe them for large sums of gold
> And send them after to supply our wants;
> For we make for Ireland presently.
> (R2.I.iv.42-52)

Richard orders his flatterers "to farm our royal realm" with "blank charters" to

meet the "liberal largess" of "too great a court," thus forcing his subjects to pay

for his excess.

> Now put it, God, in the physician's mind
> To help him to his grave immediately!
> The lining of his coffers shall make coats
> To deck our soldiers for these Irish wars.

> Come, gentlemen, let's all go visit him.
> Pray God we make haste, and come too late!
> (R2.I.iv.59-64)

Moreover, Richard openly proclaims that he hopes to help his Uncle, John of Gaunt, "to his grave immediately!" Richard does "divide the world" into camps of those with him and against him; however, this division takes place after the fall from the garden of England, and is inverted[231]. His royal family and his subjects who should be with him are alienated and pitted against him, while his flatterers support him.

Richard's next step down, after having inverted social order, is the breaking of the law. In the further search for coins to fill his coffers, Richard violates the very law that makes him king: the right of lawful succession. Immediately following Gaunt's death in Act II, scene i, Richard wants to have him dispossessed, of land, title and treasure. The Duke of York, no longer able to hold his tongue, explains what this final transgression of the law means to Richard's own title:

> How long should I be patient? Ah how long
> Shall tender duty make me suffer wrong?
> Not Gloucester's death, nor Hereford's banishment,
> Nor Gaunt's rebukes, nor England's private wrongs,
> Nor the prevention of poor Bolingbroke
> About his marriage. Nor my own disgrace,
> Have ever made me sour my patient cheek,
> Or bend one wrinkle on my Sovereign's face.
> I am the last of noble Edward's sons,
> Of whom thy father, Prince of Wales, was first:
> In war was never lion raged more fierce,
> In peace was never gentle lamb more mild,

Than was that young and princely gentleman.
...
But when he frowned, it was against the French
And not against his friends.  His noble hand
Did win what he did spend, and spent not that
Which his triumphant father's hand had won.
His hands were guilty of no kindred blood,
But guilty of the enemies of his kin.
...
Take Hereford's rights away, and take from Time
His charters and his customary rights,
Let not tomorrow then ensue today;
Be not thyself--for how art thou a king
But by fair sequence and succession?
(R2.II.i.163-75,178-83,195-9)


York mentions various other abuses that Richard has committed as king as "England's private wrongs."  Finally, York must recall the royal heritage of his father Edward III, and remind Richard that "[thou art] a king/But by fair sequence and succession."  While the phase of law represents the individual's "obligations to society," especially the king's obligation to his subjects, Richard's vision is focused down the path of the fall that he has created for himself.  He demands Gaunt's "plate, his goods, his money, and his lands," not realizing he has also forfeited his own claim to the throne (R2.II.i.209).

It is only after Richard returns from Ireland at the beginning of Act III and realizes that he is essentially powerless to stop Bolingbroke from usurping the crown, that he realizes the gravity of his actions.  Richard's wisdom again takes an inverted form as he begins to understand the consequences of his inversion of his royal responsibility. He has broken the law that forms the very foundation of his authority.  In near despair, Richard senses his mortality for the first time:

Let's talk of graves, of worms, and epitaphs,
Make dust our of paper, and with rainy eyes
Write sorrow on the bosom of the earth.
Let's chose executors and talk of wills:
And yet not so, for what can we bequeath
Save our deposèd bodies to the ground?
Our lands, our lives, and all are Bolingbroke's,
And nothing can we call our own, but death
And that small model of the barren earth
Which serves as paste and cover to our bones.
For God's sake let us sit upon the ground
And tell sad stories of the death of kings:
How some have been deposed, some slain in war,
Some haunted by the ghosts they have deposed,
Some poisoned by their wives, some sleeping killed,
All murdered--for within the hollow crown
That rounds the mortal temples of a king
Keeps Death his court, and there the antic sits,
Scoffing his state and grinning at his pomp,
Allowing him a breath, a little scene,
To monarchize, be feared, and kill with looks,
Infusing him with self and vain conceit,
As if this flesh which walls about our life
Were brass impregnable; and, humored thus,
Comes at last, and with a little pin
Bores through his castle wall, and farewell king!
Cover your heads, and mock not flesh and blood
With solemn reverence; throw away respect,
Tradition, form, and ceremonious duty;
For you have but mistook me all this while:
I live with bread like you, feel want,
Taste grief, need friends--subjected thus,
How can you say to me, I am a king?
(R2.III.ii.145-177)

Richard's realization is that Bolingbroke has broken "Tradition, form, and ceremonious duty," and "throw[n] away respect" for the king; however, with this realization comes the first awareness of his own humanity. Richard can finally "feel want,/Taste grief, need friends." While his vision is trapped in the past of what has happened, he has finally come to terms with the reality of the present.

The vision of the future, that of prophecy, only comes to Richard after he

has conceded that Bolingbroke will take his crown.  Richard's vision, still

pointing downward from his fall, sees the horrible future that awaits England if

Bolingbroke usurps the crown:

>           we thought ourself thy lawful king:
> And if we be, how dare thy joints forget
> To pay their awful duty to our presence?
> If we be not, show us the hand of God
> That hath dismissed us from our stewardship;
> For well we know no hand of blood and bone
> Can grip the sacred handle of our scepter,
> Unless he do profane, steal, or usurp;
> And though you think that all, as you have done,
> Have torn their souls by turning them from us,
> And we are barren and bereft of friends,
> Yet know, my master God omnipotent,
> Is mustering in his clouds on our behalf
> Armies of pestilence, and they shall strike
> Your children yet unborn and unbegot
> That lift your vassal hands against my head,
> And threat the glory of my precious crown.
> Tell Bolingbroke--for yon methinks he stands--
> That every stride he makes upon my land
> Is dangerous treason.  He is come to open
> The purple testament of bleeding war;
> But ere the crown he looks for live in peace
> Ten thousand bloody crowns of mothers' sons
> Shall ill become the flower of England's face,
> Change the complexion of her maid-pale peace
> To scarlet indignation, and bedew
> Her pastor's grass with faithful English blood.
> (R2.III.iii.72-99)

Richard's vision is of the bloody civil war that will lay waste to the garden

of England as "faithful English blood" soils the "flower of England's face."  He knows that he is the rightful king and that the usurpation of the throne will lead England to suffering. Because his vision is directed down, he cannot begin to see past Henry IV, and the success of Henry V at reuniting France and England. Richard predicts, however, that "God omnipotent...shall strike/Your children yet unborn and unbegot," forecasting the reign of Henry VI and the War of the Roses.

God's incarnation is in the form of making Richard realize that he must transcend his own fall (having been a type of Adam) and now become a type of Christ, accepting his plight and suffering through it. Richard, in the great deposition scene in Act IV, knows that he must surrender the crown to Bolingbroke and endures the debasement of giving away his kingship:

> Alack, why am I sent for to a king,
> Before I have shook off the regal thoughts
> Wherewith I reigned? I hardly yet have learn'd
> To insinuate, flatter, bow, and bend my knee.
> Give sorrow leave awhile to tutor me
> To this submission. Yet I will remember
> The favors of these men. Were they not mine?
> Did they not sometime cry 'all hail!' to me?
> So Judas did to Christ; but he, in twelve,
> Found truth in all but one; I in twelve thousand, none.
> ...
> some of you, with Pilate, wash your hands,
> Showing an outward pity; yet you Pilates
> Have delivered me to my sour cross,
> And water cannot wash away your sin.
> ...
> my grief lies all within,
> And these external manners of laments
> Are merely shadows to the unseen grief
> That swells with silence in the tortured soul.
> There lies the substance: and I thank thee, King,

> For thy greatest bounty, that not only giv'st
> Me cause to wail, but teachest me the way
> How to lament the cause.
> (R2.IV.i.162-71,238-241,293-301)

Richard, becoming like Christ is "delivered" to a "sour cross." Richard's spiritual crucifixion, however, finally makes him turn from "external manners" to contemplate his "tortured soul." He rejects his vanity in this world and turns toward spiritual humility.

By the end of Act V, Richard has begun to repent his sins, experiencing the "spiritual metamorphosis" that gives him "an enlarged vision of the dimensions of human life" typical of the gospel phase[232]. In his lonely cell, Richard finally realizes the implications of his actions, and is ready to accept the consequences for them:

> I have been studying how I may compare
> This prison where I live unto the world:
> And for because the world is populous,
> And here is not a creature but myself,
> I cannot do it. Yet I'll hammer it out:
> My brain I'll prove the female to my soul,
> My soul the father, and these two beget
> A generation of still-breeding thoughts;
> And these same thoughts people this little world,
> In humors like people of this world,
> For no thought is contented. The better sort,
> As thoughts of things divine are intermixed
> With scruples, and do set the word itself
> Against the word; as thus: "Come, little ones";
> And then again,
> "It is as hard to come as for a camel
> To thread the postern of a small needle's eye."
> Thoughts tending to ambition, they do plot
> Unlikely wonders: how these vain weak nails

May tear a passage thorough the flinty ribs
Of this hard world, my ragged prison walls;
...
I wasted time, now doth Time waste me:
(R2.V.v.1-21,49)


Having come to terms with his sins as king, and his humanity after being

dethroned, Richard undergoes a spiritual reawakening. The apocalyptic vision

that Richard receives, however, forces him to "fight his way out of history"

rather than "simply awaken from it"[233]. Richard's final apocalyptic trial takes

place near the end of Act V when he valiantly fights back against his assassins:


How now! What means Death in this rude assault?
Villain, thy own hand yields thy death's instrument.
[Snatches a weapon and kills one.]
Go thou, and fill another room in hell!
[He kills another.] Here Exton strikes him down.
That hand shall burn in never-quenching fire
That staggers thus my person. Exton, thy fierce hand
Hath with the King's blood stained the King's own land.
Mount, mount, my soul; thy seat is up on high,
Whilst my gross flesh sinks downward here to die.
[Dies.]
(R2.V.vi.105-12)


With Richard's death the physical world dies as his "gross flesh sinks

downward" and his soul ascends "up on high." Richard's death also condemns

the garden of England to more strife because "the King's blood [has] stained

the King's own land."

Henry IV's kingship is created from the spoken word of Richard during

Richard's incarnation in the deposition scene of *Richard II* (Act IV, scene i).

While Henry has usurped the throne, Richard knows that he must properly turn

over the crown and make Henry a proper king or England will suffer more

bloodshed.  Richard undoes himself as king in a mock anti-ceremony,

sarcastically offering Henry his position:


>     Here, cousin, seize the crown. Here, cousin,
>     On this side my hand, and on that side yours.
>     Now is this golden crown like a deep well
>     That owes two buckets, filling one another
>     The emptier dancing in the air,
>     The other down, unseen, and full of water.
>     That bucket down and full of tears am I,
>     Drinking my griefs, whilst you mount up on high.
>     ...
>             I will undo myself.
>     I give this heavy weight from off my head,
>     And this unwieldy scepter from my hand,
>     The pride of kingly sway from out my heart;
>     With mine own tears I wash away my balm,
>     With mine own hands I give away my crown,
>     With mine own tongue deny my sacred state,
>     With my own breath release all duteous oaths;
>     All pomp and majesty I do forswear;
>     My manors, rents, revenues, I forgo;
>     My acts, decrees, and statutes I deny:
>     God pardon all oaths that are broke to me,
>     God keep all vows unbroke are made to thee.
>     Make me, that nothing have, with nothing grieved,
>     And thou with all pleased, that hast all achieved.
>     Long may'st thou live in Richard's seat to sit,
>     And soon lie Richard in an earthy pit.
>     God save King Henry, unkinged Richard says,
>     And send him many years of sunshine days.
>     (R2.IV.i.181-188,202-220)


Richard mocks the ceremony that Henry has defiled and knows that he,

himself, will "soon lie [dead]...in an earthy pit."  Yet there is some sense of hope for the restoration of England when Richard acknowledges the new king, wishing him "many years of sunshine days."

Henry IV's fall seems inevitable after his violent ascension of the throne. Richard has, however, given him control of his own destiny by peacefully surrendering the crown. Henry's intentions seem clear enough when we hear from Exton that he asked, "Have I no friend will rid me of this living fear?" (R2.V.iv.2). Of course, the King's wishes are executed and Richard is assassinated. At the end or *Richard II*, however, Henry IV seem shocked to find Richard's blood on his hands:

> Lords, I protest, my soul is full of woe,
> That blood should sprinkle me to make me grow.
> Come, mourn with me for what I do lament,
> And put on sullen black incontinent.
> I'll make a voyage to the Holy Land,
> To wash this blood off from my guilty hand.
> (R2.V.vi.45-50)

To some extent Henry IV seemed justified in returning to England out of exile and taking the throne when Richard would not recognize his right of succession. Yet, Henry has taken his newly acquired power too seriously from the beginning, ordering the execution of Bushy and Green in the beginning of Act III. Now being responsible for Richard's death, and having spilled royal blood "to make me grow," Henry's experiences his fall, thrusting England deeper down into another round of revolution and civil war.

The most telling passage illustrating the phase of revolution during Henry

IV's reign is the opening passage of *Henry IV, Part 1*, where Henry voices his

concerns for the state of the kingdom:

> So shaken as we are, so wan with care,
> Find we a time for frightened peace to plant
> And breathe short-winded accents of new broils
> To be commenced in stronds afar remote.
> No more the thirsty entrance of this soil
> Shall daub her lips with her own children's blood,
> No more shall trenching war channel her fields,
> Nor bruise her flow'rets with the armèd hoofs
> Of hostile paces. Those opposéd eyes
> Which, like meteors of a troubled heaven,
> All of one nature, of one substance bred,
> Did lately meet in the intestine shock
> And furious close of civil butchery,
> Shall now in mutual well-beseeming ranks
> March all one way and be no more opposed
> Against acquaintance, kindred, and allies.
> The edge of war, like an ill-sheathèd knife,
> No more shall cut his master. Therefore, friends,
> As far as to the sepulcher of Christ—
> Whose soldier now, under whose blessèd cross
> We are impressèd and engaged to fight—
> Forthwith a power of English shall levy,
> Whose arms were molded in their mother's womb
> To chase these pagans in those holy fields
> Over whose acres walked those blessèd feet
> Which fourteen hundred years ago were nailed
> For our advantage on the bitter cross.
> (1H4.I.i.1-27)

Although Henry hopes to find "time for frightened peace to plant," he can

never get over being "So shaken...so wan with care." Henry IV's phase of

revolution attempts to reestablish social order putting a "furious close of civil

butchery" that has plagued his reign from the day of his ascension. Moreover,

Henry hopes to gather together his kingdom and "March all one way" leading

England on a crusade "To chase these pagans in those holy fields." Henry attempts throughout *Henry IV, Part 1* and *Henry IV, Part 2*, to divide "the world into those with us and those against us," to unify England and embark on a crusade; yet his fall, placing him at odds with God, thwarts these attempts throughout both plays[234].

One of Henry's most troubling concerns is his "unthrifty son" (R2.V.iii.1). This adds to the stagnation of movement toward the restoration of the garden of England throughout these plays. In order to reassert social order, Henry must first reestablish the law, particularly the law of rightful succession. In order to do this, Henry's heir to the throne, young Prince Hal, must be worthy of the crown his father has worked so hard to win and then to hold on to. Henry's priority is to teach his unlawful, prodigal son what "obligations to society" he has as an individual, and moreover, as a future king. The first obligation, as Henry explains in Act III of *Henry IV, Part 1*, is loyalty to his father the lawful king:

> For all the world,
> As thou art to this hour was Richard then
> When I from France set foot at Ravenspurgh;
> And even as I was then is Percy now.
> Now, by scepter, and my soul to boot,
> He hath more worthy interest to the state
> Than thou the shadow of succession;
> For of no right, nor color like to right,
> He doth fill fields with harness in the realm,
> Turns head against the lion's armèd jaws,
> And, being no more in debt to years than thou,
> Leads ancient lords and reverend bishops on
> To bloody battles and to bruising arms.

What never-dying honor hath he got
Against renownèd Douglas! whose high deeds,
Whose hot incursions and great name in arms
Holds from all soldiers chief majority
And military title capital
Through all the kingdoms that acknowledge Christ.
Thrice hath this Hotspur, Mars in swathling clothes,
This infant warrior, in his enterprises
Discomfited great Douglas; ta'en him once,
Enlargèd him, and made friend of him,
To fill the mouth of deep defiance up
And shake the peace and safety of our throne.
And what say you to this? Percy, Northumberland,
The Archbishop's grace of York, Douglas, Mortimer
Capitulate against us and are up.
But wherefore do I tell these news to thee?
Why, Harry, do I tell thee of my foes,
Which art my nearest and dearest enemy?
Thou that art like enough, through vassal fear,
Base inclination, and start of spleen,
To fight against me under Percy's pay,
To dog his heels and curtsy at his frowns,
To show how much thou art degenerate.
(1H4.III.ii.92-128)


Henry IV's condemnation of his son is severe, holding Hal's actions next

to the yard stick of noble Hotspur, and concluding that he does not measure up.

If Henry is to reestablish the law in his kingdom, he must first start with his son,

making Hal more than a "shadow of succession."

Henry cannot see Hal's hidden intentions to "break through the foul and

ugly mists/Of vapors that did seem to strangle him" to "imitate the sun"

(1H4.I.ii.205-6,201). Even the success at the battle of Shrewsbury is spoiled by

his son's lowly friends and his drunken riots in Eastcheap and a new threat of

rebellion. Henry's wisdom, therefore, is trapped in the despair of his disunited family and kingdom, as he expresses in Act III of *Henry IV, Part 2*:

> O sleep, O gentle sleep,
> Nature's soft nurse, how have I frightened thee,
> That thou no more wilt weigh my eyelids down
> And steep my senses in forgetfulness?
> ...
> Canst thou, O partial sleep, give thy repose
> To the wet sea-boy in an hour so rude;
> And in the calmest and most silent night,
> With all appliances and means to boot,
> Deny it to a king? Then, happy low, lie down!
> Uneasy lies the head that wears the crown.
> (2H4.III.i.4-8,26-31)

Henry IV finally comes to the same realization that Richard's wisdom brought him to: the crown is only valid when ceremony, tradition, and form have been respected. Knowing that he has violated law and ceremony by taking the throne, Henry understands his past actions for the first time and accepts the full weight of royal responsibility. Not being able to sleep while his troubled kingdom continues to be plagued with rebellion that in some ways he, himself, started, Henry knows "Uneasy lies the head that wears the crown."

With his newly acquired wisdom, Henry immediately breaks from contemplative wisdom to see for the first time the fulfillment of Richard's prophecy. At the nadir of the cycle of the royal metaphor, Henry's prophecy reflects back to Richard's and then downward predicting even more division in England:

> O God! That one might read the book of fate
> And see the revolution of the times

Make mountains level, and the continent,
Weary of solid firmness, melt itself
Into the sea; and other times to see
The beachy girdle of the ocean
Too wide for Neptune's hips; how chances mock
And change fills the cup of alteration
With divers liquors! O, if this were seen,
The happiest youth, viewing his progress through,
What perils past, what crosses to ensue,
Would shut the book, and sit him down and die.
'Tis not ten years gone
Since Richard and Northumberland, great friends,
Did feast together, and in two years after
Were they at wars. It is but eight years since
This Percy was the man nearest my soul,
Who like a brother toiled in my affairs
And laid his love and life under my foot,
Yea, for my sake, even to the eyes of Richard
Gave him defiance...
When Richard, with his eye brimful of tears,
Then checked and rated by Northumberland,
Did speak these words, now proved a prophecy:
"Northumberland, thou ladder by the which
My cousin Bolingbroke ascends my throne"--
Though then, God knows, I had no such intent,
But that I and greatness were compelled to kiss--
"The time shall come," thus did he follow it,
"The time shall come that foul sin, gathering head,
Shall break into corruption." So went on,
Foretelling this same time's condition
And the division of our amity.
(2H4.III.i.45-79)

Henry's vision is limited by the "revolutions of the times" which taint his reading of "the book of fate." Knowing how well Richard's prophecies have come true, for Northumberland has led the rebellion against his one time friend and ally Henry IV, Henry's prophecy looks beyond the reign of his son and sees the War of the Roses.

What has troubled Henry most throughout his reign has been the thwarting of his plans for a crusade to the Holy Land. To Henry it seems that God's intervention in history has been to prevent him from washing his hands of Richard's blood as punishment for usurping the crown. With the rebellion having being put down by Prince John, Henry hopes, near the end of Act IV, that God's intervention will finally have a different effect:

> Now, lords, if God doth give successful end
> To this debate that bleedeth at our doors,
> We will our youth lead on to higher fields
> And draw no swords but what are sanctified.
> (2H4.IV.iv.1-4)

Although God does restore peace to Henry's England, his incarnation will not go so far as to let the king lead a crusade. On his death-bed, however, Henry IV, is able to impart the gospel to his son, soon to be his successor:

> Come hither, Harry, sit thou by my bed,
> And hear, I think, the very latest counsel
> That ever I shall breathe. God knows, my son,
> By what bypaths and indirect crooked ways
> ! met this crown, and I myself know well
> How troublesome it sat upon my head.
> To thee it shall descend with better quiet,
> Better opinion, better confirmation,
> For all the soil of the achievement goes
> With me into the earth. It seemed in me
> But as an honor snatched with boisterous hand
> And I had many living to upbraid
> My gain of it by their assistance,
> Which daily grew to quarrel and to bloodshed
> Wounding supposèd peace. All these bold fears
> Thou seest with peril I have answered,
> For all my reign hath been but as a scene

Acting that argument. And now my death
Changes the mood, for what in me was purchased
Falls upon thee in a more fairer sort,
So though thou stand'st more sure than I could do,
Thou art not firm enough, since griefs are green.
And all my friends, which thou must make thy friends,
Have but their stings and teeth newly ta'en out,
By whose fell working I was first advanced
And by whose power I well might lodge a fear
To be again displaced. Which to avoid,
I cut them off, and had a purpose now
To lead out many to the Holy Land,
Lest rest and lying still might make them look
Too near unto my state. Therefore, my Harry,
Be it thy course to busy giddy minds
With foreign quarrels, that action, hence borne out,
May waste the memory of the former days.
More would I, but my lungs are wasted so
That strength of speech is utterly denied me.
How I came by the crown, O God forgive,
And grant it may with thee in true peace live!
(2H4.IV.v.181-219)


Henry IV tells his son the good news that the troubles of the kingdom

caused by the "crooked ways/I met this crown," will go "with me into the earth."

For Hal the crown shall "descend with better quiet,/ Better opinion, better

confirmation." The law of rightful succession has been restored. Having finally

returned social order to England, Henry also advises his son on how to

maintain it: "busy giddy minds/With foreign quarrels, that action, hence borne

out,/May waste the memory of the former days." In Henry's gospel he hopes

his son may avoid the follies he has created.

Still at the bottom of the royal metaphor cycle, Henry IV's apocalypse is

anticlimactic. Having finally restored England to peace and order, he has the "revelation" that he will never enjoy the glory of God that he hoped a crusade might bring his people[235]. Instead, he realizes the irony of his death:

> Laud be to God! Even there my life must end.
> It hath been prophesied to me many years
> I should not die but "in Jerusalem,"
> Which vainly I supposed the Holy Land.
> But bear me to that chamber; there I'll lie.
> In that "Jerusalem" shall Harry die.
> (2H4.IV.v.235-40)

The ascension of young Henry V takes place at the end of *Henry IV, Part 2*, finally allowing the young prince to throw off his cloak of darkness and shine like the sun. Ironically, it has been the darker side of Hal's development as a Prince that has created the monarch who will become the ideal Christian king. At the beginning of *Henry V*, the Bishop of Ely describes Henry's creation with garden imagery:

> The strawberry grows underneath the nettle,
> And wholesome berries thrive and ripen best
> Neighbored by fruit of baser quality;
> And so the Prince obscured his contemplation
> Under the veil of wilderness, which (no doubt)
> Grew like the summer grass, fastest by night,
> Unseen, yet crescive in his faculty.
> (H5.I.i.60-6)

The emphasis of Henry V's creation is on his "wholesome" nature, despite his growth "Under the veil of wilderness." The prodigal son, raised near "fruit of baser quality," has returned a new man. The curve of the royal metaphor is working its way up as this new king brings hope to his reborn country.

Henry V's fall, because of his ascension toward restoring England, is an inverted fall or an anti-fall. The Archbishop of Canterbury recognizes this anti-fall, in the first scene of *Henry V*:

> The courses of his youth promised it not.
> The breath no sooner left his father's body
> But that this wilderness, mortified in him,
> Seemed to die too; yea, at that very moment,
> Consideration like an angel came
> And whipped th' offending Adam out of him,
> Leaving his body as a paradise
> T'envelop and contain celestial spirits.
> Never was such a sudden scholar made;
> Never came reformation in a flood
> With such a heady currance scouring faults;
> (H5.I.i.24-34)

Henry V's immediate acceptance of this new role when his father dies was not predicted by anyone who knew of his riotous youth. Yet it was "this wilderness, mortified in him" that "whipped th' offending Adam out of him," causing his anti-fall. For Henry "reformation came in a flood" that washed his offensive sins clean and gave him the competence of a "sudden scholar," despite the fact that "his youth promised it not."

Having fallen upward in a sense, Henry V resolves to fulfill his father's dream of finally uniting England in a single cause for the glory of God. Embracing his father's words of gospel, Henry V "divides the world into those with us and those against us"[236]. His sights are set on France, noting an ancestral claim that indicates those lands should be part of the great kingdom of England. Henry recognizes that "those with right beliefs or attitudes [will] emerge on top with their now powerful enemies rendered impotent," and therefore asks the question "May I with right and conscience make this claim?" (H5.I.ii.96)[237]. It is the Archbishop of Canterbury who reassures Henry of the righteousness of his cause, in God's eyes, to campaign in France:

> Gracious lord,
> Stand for your own, unwind your bloody flag,
> Look back into your mighty ancestors;
> Go, my dread lord, to your great-grandsire's tomb,
> From whom you claim; invoke his warlike spirit,
> And your great-uncle's, Edward the Black Prince,
> Who on the French ground played a tragedy,
> Making defeat on the full power of France,
> Whiles his most mighty father on a hill
> Stood smiling, to behold his lion's whelp
> Forage in blood of French nobility.
> O noble English, that could entertain
> With half their forces the full pride of France,
> And let another half stand laughing by,
> All out of work, and cold for action!
> (H5.I.ii.103-14)

The Archbishop's words indicate that his cause is just, but his tone also speaks of a confident, united England that "could entertain/With half their forces the full pride of France." Moreover, Canterbury's rhetoric invokes Henry's proud royal lineage as a reminder of England past glory. Henry's ultimate decision to "let every man now task his thought/That this fair action may on feet be brought" indicates the "revolutionary context" of this passage in which "[t]he word listened to and acted upon is the starting point of a course of action" (H5.I.ii.309-10)[238].

Before Henry V's expedition can leave for France, the three traitors,
Scroop, Cambridge, and Grey, are caught. Their betrayal represents the last
unlawful act against the King. Henry, after feigning mercy, is swift in his
restoration of the law, ordering their arrest:

> Treason and Murder ever kept together
> As two yoke-devils sworn to either's purpose,
> ...
> Such and so finely bolted didst thou seem;
> And thus thy fall hath left a kind of blot
> To mark the full-fraught man and best indued
> With some suspicion. I will weep for thee;
> For this revolt of thine, methinks, is like
> Another fall of man. Their faults are open.
> Arrest them to the answer of the law;
> And God acquit them of their practices!
> (H5.II.ii.105-6,137-43)

Henry has no sympathy for their "fall" that would "mark the full-fraught
man and best indued/With some suspicion." Henry demands that they receive
the "answer of the law," indicating that their transgression will be punished.
Henry's stern enforcement of the law, even against his close friend Scroop,
indicates that law in England has been unequivocally restored, and that a
unified and lawful England will not betray the King while he is in France.

After campaigning for months, Henry's troops are tired and worn down,
but have fought well in France. Rather than walk away from a fight, Henry
squares off against the French at Agincourt. The night before the engagement
the vastly outnumbered English know they will encounter fresh French forces in
the morning. During the night, Henry V wanders, disguised, through his camp.

Only after talking with his men and contemplating the inevitable struggle of the

morning does he gain the vision of wisdom:

"Upon the King! Let us our lives, our souls,
Our debts, our careful wives,
Our children, and our sins, lay on the King!"
We must bear all. O hard condition,
Twin-born with greatness, subject to the breath
Of every fool, whose sense no more can feel
But his own wringing! What infinite heart's-ease
Must kings neglect that private men enjoy!
And what have kings that privates have not too,
Save ceremony, save general ceremony?
And what art thou, thou idol Ceremony?
What kind of god art thou, that suffer'st more
Of mortal griefs than do thy worshippers?
What are thy rents? What are thy comings-in?
O ceremony, show me but thy worth!
What is thy soul of adoration?
Art thou aught else but place, degree, and form,
Creating awe and fear in other men?
Wherein thou art less happy, being feared,
Than they in fearing.
What drink'st thou oft, instead of homage sweet,
But poisoned flattery? O, be sick, great greatness,
And bid thy ceremony give thee cure!
Thinks thou the fiery fever will go out
With titles blown from adulation?
Will it give place to flexure and low bending?
Canst thou, when thou command'st the beggar's knee,
Command the health of it? No, thou proud dream,
That play'st so subtly with a king's repose.
I am a king that find thee; and I know
'Tis not the balm, the scepter, and the ball,
The sword, the mace, the crown imperial,
The intertissued robe of gold and pearl,
The farcèd title running fore the king,
The throne he sits on, nor the tide of pomp
That beats upon the high shore of this world--
No, not all these, thrice--gorgeous ceremony
Not all these, laid in bed majestical,
Can sleep so soundly as the wretched slave,

Who, with a body filled, and vacant mind,
Gets him to rest, crammed with distressful bread;
Never sees horrid night, the child of hell;
But like the lackey, from the rise to set,
Sweats in the eye of Phoebus, and all night
Sleeps in Elysium; next day after dawn,
Doth rise and help Hyperion to his horse;
And follows so the ever-running year
With profitable labor to his grave;
And but for ceremony, such a wretch,
Winding up days with toil and nights with sleep,
Had the forehand and vantage of a king,
The slave, a member of the country's peace,
Enjoys it; but in gross brain little wots
What watch the king keeps to maintain the peace,
Whose hours the peasant best advantages.
...
O God of battles, steel my soldier's hearts,
Possess them not with fear! Take from them now
The sense of reck'ning, or th' opposèd numbers
Pluck their hearts from them. Not today, O Lord
O, not today, think not upon the fault
My father made in compassing the crown!
I Richard's body have interred new,
And on it have bestowed more contrite tears
Than from it issued forcèd drops of blood.
Five hundred poor I have in yearly pay,
Who twice a day their withered hands hold up
Towards heaven, to pardon blood;
And I have built two chantries,
Where the sad and solemn priests sing still
For Richard's soul. More will I do:
Though all that I can do is nothing worth;
Since that my penitence comes after all.
Imploring pardon.
(H5.IV.i.235-289,294-311)

Henry sees, as his father and Richard before him have done, that it is

the king that must "bear all" for his subjects and his country. He now realizes

that it is only "Ceremony" that separates him from other men and that only the form, tradition, and heritage of ceremony can give him the strength to lead his

men in the morning.  Henry ends his contemplation with a prayer, prudently

asking God to "think not upon the fault/My father made in compassing the

crown."  Henry, embracing wisdom, asks that the festering wounds of the past

plaguing England before his reign as king be healed before battle, "Imploring

pardon" from God.

In the morning, Henry V's prayers serve him well, as now he can see,

like a prophet, the victory and glory for England that the day will bring.  In an

effort to motivate his troops Henry shares his vision of Glory with his men:

> If we are marked to die, we are enow
> To do our country loss; and if to live,
> The fewer men, the greater share of honor.
> God's will! I pray thee wish not one man more.
> By Jove, I am not covetous for gold,
> Nor care I who doth feed upon my cost;
> It yeams me not if men my garments wear;
> Such outward things dwell not in my desires;
> But if it be a sin to covet honor,
> I am the most offending soul alive.
> No, faith, my coz, wish not a man from England.
> God's peace! I would not lose so great an honor
> As one man more methinks would share from me
> For the best hope I have. O, do not wish one more!
> Rather proclaim it, Westmoreland, through my host,
> That he which hath no stomach to this fight,
> Let him depart; his passport shall be made,
> And crowns for convoy put into his purse;
> We would not die in that man's company
> That fears his fellowship to die with us.
> This day is called the Feast of Crispian:
> He that outlives this day, and comes safe home,
> Will stand a-tiptoe when this day is named.
> And rouse him at the name of Crispian.
> He that shall see this day, and live old age,

Will yearly on the vigil feast his neighbors
And say, "Tomorrow is Saint Crispian."
Then will he strip his sleeve and show his scars,
And say, "These wounds I had on Crispin's day."
Old men forget; yet all shall be forgot,
But he'll remember, with advantages,
What feats he did that day. Then shall our names,
Familiar in his mouth as household words--
Harry the King, Bedford and Exeter,
Warwick and Talbot, Salisbury and Gloucester--
Be in their flowing cups freshly rememb'red.
This story shall the good man teach his son;
And Crispin Crispian shall ne'er go by,
From this day to the ending of the world,
But we in it shall be remember'd--
We few, we happy few, we band of brothers;
For he today that sheds his blood with me
Shall be my brother; be he ne'er so vile,
This day shall gentle his condition.
And gentlemen in England, now abed,
Shall think themselves accursed they were not here;
And hold their manhoods cheap whiles any speaks
That fought with us upon Saint Crispin's day.
(H5.IV.iii.20-67)

Henry predicts that "He that outlives this day, and comes safe home...From this day to the ending of the world...shall be remembered" for bringing God's glory on the English. It is only after the battle of Agincourt, however, that Henry truly understands how great a victory he and his tired compatriots have won. Upon hearing numbers of French and English dead at the end of Act IV, Henry realizes that God's intervention played a hand in the victory, proclaiming:

O God, thy arm was here!
And not to us, but to thy name alone
Ascribe we all. When, without stratagem,

> But in plain shock and even play of battle,
> Was ever known so great and little loss
> On one part and on th' other? Take it, God,
> For it is none but thine!
> ...
> Let there be sung "Non nobis" and "Te Deum,"
> The dead with charity enclosed in clay,
> And then to Calais; and to England then;
> Where ne'er from France arrived more happy men.
> (H5.IV.viii.108-13,125-129)

Henry believes the victory at Agincourt could only have been won with "so great and little loss" if God had willed it. The moment appears to be "one of those dialectical confrontations in which history suddenly expands to myth and indicates a dimension beyond the historical"[239]. Henry V's pious response comes from what he believes to be the incarnation, or human manifestation, of God's will. Such a victory over the French justifies Henry's declaration of the justness of his cause in Act I.

For the French to be defeated by such lopsided numbers must mean they "were trying to block the activity of God" in the form of Henry V's quest to reunite the kingdoms of France and England. Such a victory for Henry, therefore, reassures him of having won the greater glory of God in combat. The defeat for the French, however, suggests that their resistance was against not only the English, but God's will. In Act V, scene ii, the Duke of Burgundy realizes the suffering of his country has been due to France's thwarting of God's will. He speaks in gospel-like words:

> Peace

Dear nurse of arts, plenties, and joyful births,
Should not, in this best garden of the world,
Our fertile France, put up her lovely visage.
Alas, she hath from France too long been chased!
And all her husbandry doth lie on heaps,
Corrupting in it own fertility.
Her vine, the merry cheerer of the heart,
Unprunèd dies; her hedges even-pleached,
Like prisoners wildly overgrown with hair,
Put forth disordered twigs; her fallow leas
The darnel, hemlock, and the rank fumitory
Doth root upon, while that the coulter rusts
That should deracinate such savagery;
The even mead, that erst brought sweetly forth
The freckled cowslip, burnet, and green clover,
Wanting the scythe, all uncorrected, rank,
Conceives by idleness, and nothing teems
But hateful docks, rough thistles, kecksies, burrs,
Losing both beauty and utility.
And as our vineyards, fallows, meads, and hedges,
Defective in their natures, grow to wildness;
Even so our houses and ourselves and children
Have lost, or do not learn for want of time,
The sciences that should become our country;
But grow, like savages--as soldiers will,
That nothing do but meditate on blood--
To swearing and stern looks, diffused attire,
And everything that seems unnatural.
Which to reduce into our former favor
You are assembled; and my speech entreats
That I may know the let why gentle Peace
Should not expel these inconveniences,
And bless us with her former qualities.
(H5.V.ii.36-67)


Burgundy's gospel is a plea for a reconciliation between the "too

long...chased" garden of "fertile France" and England.  Burgundy's realization is

that France alone is being corrupted "in it own fertility," which "seems

unnatural."  Only "gentle Peace" in a marriage between France and England can restore "her former qualities." With this marriage "plagues, wars, [and]

famines" of the English invasion will end in the "eventual transformation...of the

world into a new heaven and earth" during the apocalypse[240].

The apocalypse at the end of *Henry V* brings "the destruction of the way

of seeing order" to the French[241]. Instead France is forced to compromise and

acquiesce to God's will of a holy marriage "'twixt England and fair France"

(H5.V.ii.367). The Queen of France recognizes this in her monologue that

closes the last scene of the play.

> God, the best maker of all marriages,
> Combine your hearts in one, your realms in one!
> As man and wife, being two, are one in love,
> So be there 'twixt your kingdoms such a spousal
> That never may ill office, or jealousy,
> Which troubles oft the bed of blessed marriage,
> Thrust in between the paction of these kingdoms
> To make divorce of their incorporate league;
> That English may as French, French Englishmen,
> Receive each other! God speak this Amen!
> (H5.V.ii.371-380)

The Queen's blessing, then, is the final "revelation" of God's divine plan,

where "the people of God are raised into recognition"[242]. The vision of history

now has new meaning, leading up to the "restoration of the tree and the water

of life, the two elements of the original creation"[243]. We find out in the epilogue

to *Henry V* that Henry V achieved "the world's best garden," (H5.Ep.7) marking

the restoration of both England and France to a renewed state of creation and

prosperity for the people of both kingdoms. This epilogue also mentions, however, that, as Richard predicted, "Armies of pestilence...shall strike/Your children yet unborn and unbegot" (R2.III.iii.86-7). Henry VI will lose France and make "England bleed" (H5.Ep.12) again. After restoring England to her former glory before Richard's fall, Henry V cannot prevent culpable man from falling again and making his country suffer through civil strife.

While all of these narrative "nodes" attempt to represent the typological phases that the kings experience as England progresses down and then up again on the curve of the royal metaphor, they do not "fit" into perfect patterns. Even after being given the imagery and events of each typological phase, considering the development of the royal metaphor throughout the four plays, and establishing the nodal criteria noted at the beginning of this section, it is still an enigmatic process to locate these nodes. Certainly there are debatable alternatives to some of them; however, this particular pattern of typological nodes does illuminate some of the major tensions and ideas in these plays while still illustrating the existence of Biblical, typological cycles. If, however, alternatives are found and pieced together, which certainly can be done, the major point of this paper will have been proven: Biblical typological cycles do function in Shakespeare's *Henriad*.

At this point this paper has met its intended goal of examining the "great code" in Shakespeare's *Henriad*. Frye's typological, narrative phase model, however, has failed to even recognize some of the most important characters and events in the *Henriad*, the most significant of which is Falstaff. Frye's cycle also cannot account for young Prince Hal's relationships with his father,

Falstaff, Hotspur, and the Chief Justice that helps him develop into the ideal

Christian monarch.  These large gaps are the fatal flaw in this critical approach

to understanding the *Henriad* through Biblical narrative cycles.

Frye's hypothesis that the "great code" in the Bible and Western

literature is typology is correct.  Why, then, is it that Frye's Biblical, typological,

narrative patterns cannot capture the meaning of the *Henriad*?

## PART III - THE TRIADIC: A TENTATIVE CONCLUSION

At the end of Part II of this paper the question was asked as to why Frye's Biblical, typological, narrative patterns could not capture the meaning of Shakespeare's *Henriad*. Before an answer to that question can be formulated, however, there necessarily needs to be some discussion of a theory of language and criticism.

I.    A THEORY OF LANGUAGE

A. THE PERCY FACTOR: WALKER PERCY AND LANGUAGE

My first glimmer of understanding as to why Northrop Frye's typological phase model could not fully encompass Shakespeare's *Henriad* came after I read the literary essays of contemporary American novelist Walker Percy. In his three books of literary essays, *The Message in the Bottle*, *Lost in the Cosmos*, and *Signposts in a Strange Land*, Percy explores the use of "signs" in language. What Percy is examining is the question of "semiotics" which he defines as "the science which deals with signs and the use of them by other creatures," or more specifically, "the human use of signs"[244].

Semiotics is a field that "runs the risk of being about everything and hence about nothing" because so many philosophers and thinkers have defined and redefined semiotics in so many diverse ways[245]. Percy narrows his study of semiotics to specific individuals who he believes have been helpful in identifying how meaning is transmitted through language. These individuals including: Ernst Cassirer, who studied "the many fold ways in which man uses the symbol [the sign], in language, myth, and art, as his primary means of articulating reality;" Charles S. Pierce, who founded "the modern discipline of semiotics" and was "the first to distinguish clearly between 'dyadic' behavior of stimulus-response sequences and the 'triadic' character of symbol [sign] use;" Ferdinand de Saussure, who analyzed "the human sign as the union of the signifier (*significant*) and the signified (*signifié*);" Hans Werner, who "explored the process in which the signified is articulated within the form of the signifier;" and Susanne K. Langer, "who, from the posture of behavioral science, clearly set forth the qualitative difference between animals' use of signals and man's use of symbols [signs]"[246]. Even amongst these philosophers there is a diverse use of semiotics vocabulary, thus what some might call "symbols" are what Percy calls "signs."

In most of his literary essays, Percy is moving toward an understanding of how human beings communicate using "signs." What I hope to gain from studying the writings of Walker Percy is a better understanding of what Northrop Frye means when he says:

> The cultural aura, or whatever it is, that insulates us from nature consists among other things of words, and the verbal part of it is what I call mythology, or the total structure of human creation conveyed by words, with literature at its center[247].

Walker Percy and Northrop Frye are both addressing the same enigmatic "problem" of how words create meaning for human beings. Frye would say that meaning is transmitted through "myth" ("*mythos*" or "narrative"), the way in which "words [are] arranged in a sequential order"[248]. Percy would say that meaning is transmitted through "signs," broken up into two elements a "signifier" and a "signified"[249]. Both Percy and Frye, however, would agree that meaning is conveyed in words and verbal structures that make up the "signs" and "myths" that other human beings interpret and understand.

Without going into the extensive depths of Percy's exploration of semiotics, it is my goal in the last part of this paper to establish some connections between what Northrop Frye is describing through mythology and what Walker Percy is exploring through semiotics.

## B. SCIENTIFIC UNDERSTANDING: DYADIC, OBJECTIVE

Earlier in this paper, I examined how causality worked and why it was essentially a scientific process. This notion of causality came from Northrop Frye's description of how metaphor works in time, causality being a backwards movement from "effect" to "cause" to ascribe meaning to events[250]. I also explained how Frye describes myth and metaphor as belonging "to the mirror, not the window," indicating the inherently subjective bias of language[251].

These are the same issues that Walker Percy addresses in his literary essays. Percy first addresses the "dyadic" or scientific approach to understanding, which uses causal thinking in an attempt to reach an objective understanding of an observation. As Charles Pierce first described it, a "dyadic" relationship involves "physical forces...between pairs of particles"[252]. Percy explains an example of a dyadic relationship:

> If A throws B away and B hits C in the eye, this event may be
> understood in terms of two dyadic relations, one between A and B,
> the other between B and C[253].

The most important aspect of this dyadic relationship is that each element in a larger problem can "be reduced to a series of dyadic relations" that as Pierce says "takes place between two subjects...or at any rate is a resultant action between pairs"[254]. Typical "[d]yadic events" are "energy exchanges conventionally studied by the natural sciences: subatomic particles colliding, chemical reactions, actions of force-fields on bodies, physical and chemical transactions across biological membranes, discharges, etc"[255].

Again, these dyadic relations function causally, "from cause to effect"[256]. Even more complicated relations are still dyadic, for example the chemist who pours chemical A into a glass with chemical B, which then forms compound C. A reacts with B which leads to C. A does not combine with B mysteriously to create C, because the chemist knows that when A and B react, their components necessarily form C. Each step is a causal relationship. The cause of mixing A and B leads to the effect C. In many ways this series of dyadic relationships is similar to Hegelian logic that moves from the cause of "thesis" to the effect of "antithesis" and then again from the cause of "antithesis" to the effect of "synthesis."

Moreover, a dyadic relationship can only be seen from an objective vantage point, as an objective observer watches A mix with B and sees the formation of C. In science there is no accounting for the chemist who pours A and B together because he is an objective factor that does not play a part in the relationships of A, B and C. Figure 3 illustrates a simple dyadic or causal relationship. This idea is exactly what Northrop Frye has in mind when he writes about causality: a type appears to cause an antitype.

In reality we know that causality works from the observation of effect or antitype to which a cause or type is later ascribed. In many ways this is precisely how science determines that when A and B are mixed they form C. At some point compound C is observed after mixing A and B, and then the

Figure 3: The Dyadic or Causal Relationship, Cause -> Effect

CAUSALITY

CAUSE AND EFFECT

"DYADIC"

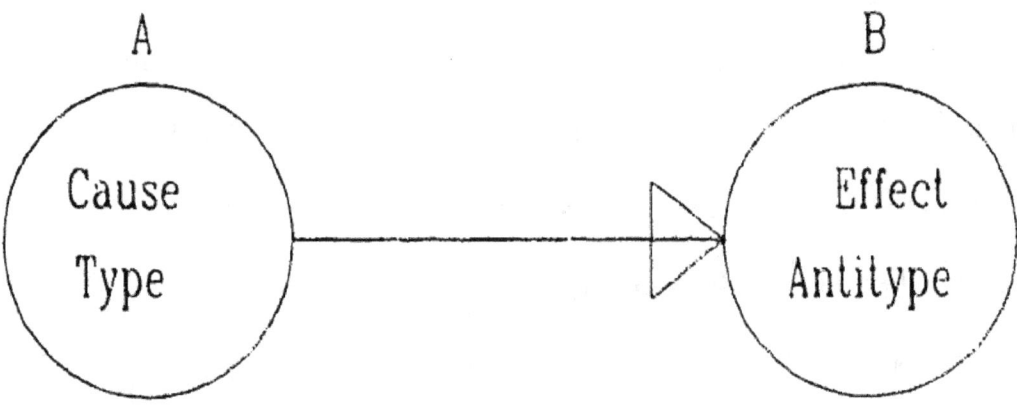

effect C is ascribed to the cause of mixing A and B. Again, the movement of ascribing meaning is backwards, and apparently objective, in the same way that modern history, using scientific methodology, attempts to understand the past as discussed earlier in this paper.

The problem with causal, dyadic, or classical scientific thinking is that it attempts to get at literal "fact" rather than "true" meaning. Peirce asks the question, "What is fact?"; but rather than answer it directly he points out "something which must be excluded from the category of fact...the general, and with it the permanent or eternal" (that which is "true")[257]. Fact derived from a causal (or dyadic) relationship is specific and deterministic, A always leads to B; one can never convey any greater meaning through a causal relationship because the end, B, is already fixed by the specific circumstances of the relationship between A and B. A causal (or dyadic) thought process, then, can never explore meaning beyond the surface or literal understanding that a classical mechanical model can provide. And the classical mechanical model is based on "the principle of causality" that, as Ernest Nagal indicates in his book *The Structure of Science: Problems in the Logic of Scientific Exploration*, is "extremely difficult if not hopeless to regard...as a universally valid indicative truth concerning the pervasive order of events and processes"[258].

## C. LINGUISTIC UNDERSTANDING: TRIADIC SUBJECTIVE

Percy believes that "[l]ike Newtonian mechanics, dyadic theory can account for perhaps 98 per cent of natural phenomena"[259]. Unfortunately, just as classical Newtonian mechanics cannot account for the Heisenberg Uncertainty Principle, "the phenomena of talking-and-listening," the occurrence of language, also "falls in the remaining 2 percent"[260]. Even though this discussion is about language and myth, the Heisenberg Uncertainty Principle is an appropriate starting point.

"[E]nunciated by Werner Heisenberg in 1927," the Uncertainty Principle says that if we attempt to establish "the position and motion of [an] electron with precision...we shall see that *it is impossible to make these two measurements simultaneously with unlimited accuracy*"[261]. The reason that classical Newtonian physics cannot account for the Uncertainty Principle is the same reason that language does not fall into 98 per cent of most natural phenomenon; the Uncertainty Principal and language both have a "'noncausal' or 'indeterministic' structure"[262]. The nature of this noncausal or indeterministic structure in physics is that "the interactions of objects measured and measuring instruments" or the "classical distinctions between 'observed' and 'observer' cannot be maintaine[d] in subatomic physics except in an arbitrary manner"[263]. In other words, there can never be an objective observer analyzing the position or velocity of an electron. In fact, the very idea of objectivity is called into question by the Uncertainty Principle.

This is precisely the point about language that both Northrop Frye and Walker Percy make. Language operates subjectively. The subjective individual either speaking and creating meaning or hearing and understanding meaning must necessarily be factored into the equation. This idea is also precisely what Charles Pierce implies in his "triadic theory of signs"[264].

Pierce defines a "triadic" relationship as "an action, or influence, which is, or involves a cooperation of *three* subjects...this tri-relative influence not being in any way resolvable into actions between pairs"[265]. Based on Peirce's "triadic" model, Percy compares his earlier example of a dyadic relation where A throws B and hits C with a "genuine triadic relation" in which "A *gives* B to C"[266]. Peirce explains that "every genuine triadic relation involves meaning" and that "the idea of meaning is irreducible to those of quality and reaction" that occur in causal or dyadic processes[267].

Pulling together the ideas on the nature of how language conveys meaning through the works of Northrop Frye, Walker Percy, and Charles Peirce, I have synthesized a theory of language that attempts to answer the question of how subjective language transmits meaning through verbal narrative structures (that Frye would call myth) triadically.

To understand how language transmits meaning one must first recognize that language involves the subjective individual who must necessarily be part of the equation. The second step is to realize that language operates triadically, where meaning is irreducible to cause and effect type relationships. The third step is understanding that language (or as Frye would say myth) is a sign that has a "dual nature"[268]. This last point comes from Saussure who expounded the idea that '[i]n a sign, the signifier and signified are interpenetrated[269]. [A speculation--is this understanding of the "dual nature" of signs similar to the understanding of the "dual nature" of electrons that exhibit characteristics of both waves and particles in the theory of Quantum Mechanics of which the Heisenberg Uncertainty Principle is part?]

From these ideas I have ironically developed scientific models that help show how language operates triadically to convey meaning and "truth." The first mode, as illustrated in Figure 4, is of the basic components that make up the triad of language. Language is composed of elements, the subjective individual creating it and the sign that is created. The sign, however, has a dual nature and is composed of Saussure's signifier and signified. The subjective individual lives in a subjective reality of language. He creates a word or a verbal structure (Frye's narrative myth) that is a signal, but that has a dual nature, that of the word itself and that of the idea or metaphysical reality that the word or verbal structure stands for or means. These three elements make up language.

Communication also operates triadically, but because there are two subjective individuals involved, there are two triads. In Figure 5 the relationship between these two triads is seen. Subjective individual A creates a sign made up of a verbal structure and a posited metaphysical reality. Subject B hears the

Figure 4: The Triadic Nature of Language

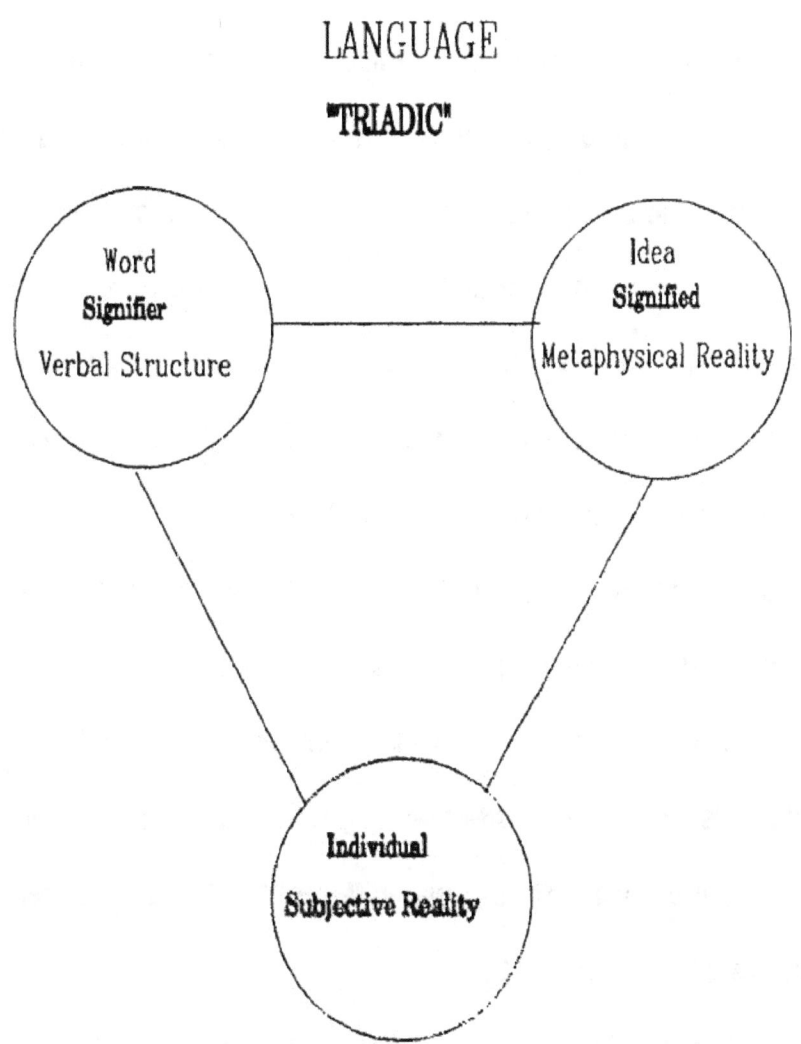

sign and understands the verbal structure and can then understand the posited metaphysical reality or idea.

Breakdown in communication can occur in many places. When A creates a verbal structure, the sign may be garbled or in a different language, in which case B cannot understand the signifier. The sign may be received by B and the signifier understood; however, A's metaphysical reality may not match B's, in which case the signified is not understood. An example of the first case would occur if A, who cannot speak French was asked a question in French by B. A cannot understand the sign created by B because he cannot understand the signifier. An example of the second would occur if A says to B, "Let's go do something fun" and B, who understands the signifiers, says to A "Okay;" but while sitting in the theater watching *Richard II*, B says to A "I thought you said we were going to do something *fun*." B later tells A that he "understood" the word "fun" to mean something physical like playing softball. B has misinterpreted A's sign by not understanding what "fun" signifies for A. The idea or metaphysical reality of "fun" was different for A than the idea or metaphysical reality of "fun" for B.

It is in this type of miscommunication that subjectivity plays its most significant role. Frye's notion of "sign" that is transmitted through language and therefore communication is what he "loosely call[s] sense, the relation of many signifiers to a common signified"[270]. The communication of meaning therefore depends on a community of people having a common metaphysical

Figure 5: The Triadic Nature of Communication

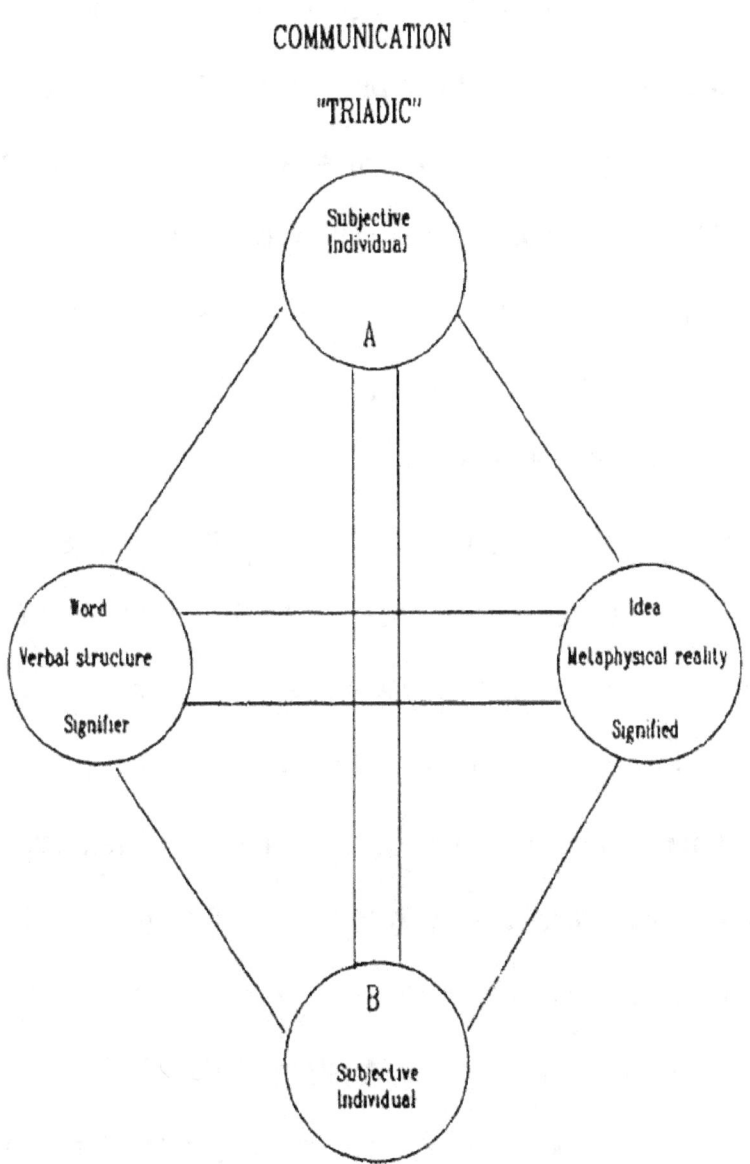

understanding of the signified realities created by verbal signifiers. Although the nature and employment of language is a subjective process, a "permanent or eternal" signified meaning can create an "objective truth," a meaning that is accepted as a metaphysical reality for a community of people. Yet precisely because language is subjective, it can be abused. The tendency of the scientific man is to first of all pretend language is an objective process in order to see the world objectively, and secondly to redefine and relegate any signifier that possesses an "objective truth" to a relative understanding of "fact" that can be proven by science. Although the scientist will not admit to it, "language is not a machine or invention that man uses, but something that, in its full range, uses man, man being ultimately the servant rather than the master of language"[271]. Frye titles his second book on the Bible and literature *Words with Power*, focusing on the idea that language has the unique ability to either unify or divide people, and that the "words with power" in the Bible actually unify Western civilization by imbuing them with a common understanding of language through the myth and metaphor conveyed in Biblical narrative. The myth and metaphor in the Bible once created a metaphysical reality in the creative imagination of all who experienced the Western, Judeo-Christian heritage. The Bible, therefore, acted at one time as a common signified idea or metaphysical reality that Western world once possessed. It was once an "objective truth."

The influx of scientific empiricism, however, has broken up the Biblical knowledge that once posited a common signified for the West, and replaced it with a relative understanding of words that can only be signified by scientifically provable "facts." Richard Weaver in his philosophical work *Ideas Have Consequences* reminds us, however, that "[w]here fact is made the criteria, knowledge has been rendered unattainable"[272]. Weaver points out that "[a]ll metaphysical community depends on the ability of men to understand one another"[273]. Because "words have power to define and compel," the common signified that the myth and metaphor of the Bible represents once held the "metaphysical community" of Western society together[274]. Unfortunately the scientific tendency of our world to search for fact rather than truth is trying "to strip words of all meaning"[275]. What replaces the common signified in language and communication is the relative. Frye reminds us that an understanding of myth, narrative, and ultimately language is "determined largely by [one's] own cultural context"[276]. When the cultural context of the individual supersedes the metaphysical community's understanding of "objective truth," language's ability to convey meaning is destroyed. Any words that once had a commonly signified metaphysical meaning are lost.

II.    A THEORY OF CRITICISM

A. HOW THE ARTISTS CONVEYS MEANING THROUGH LITERATURE

Literature conveys meaning in much the same way as does

communication.  The medium of literature is language, and therefore this

transaction should occur triadically.  In communication, two subjective

individuals are talking and listening alternately, each hoping to comprehend the

other's signs, both signifier and signified.  In the process of communication

through literature a subjective artist creates a sign consisting of a signifier, a

work of literature, that posits a signified, the meaning or metaphysical reality of

the literature.  A subjective reader then reads the work of literature and if he

can understand the signified metaphysical reality posited in the work, he will

grasp the meaning of the piece of literature.  This process is illustrated in

Figure 6.

With this model in mind, consider the case of a subjective reader outside

the Judeo-Christian Heritage, who knows nothing of the West and reads

Dante's *Divine Comedy*.  Even if the signifiers were in the same language for

both the artist and the reader, the common signified would not exist and little or

no meaning would be conveyed.  Reconsider, then, the importance of the Bible

as what Frye calls our "cultural genetic code"[277].  Even as a point of reference

then in our common understanding of the signified, the Bible plays an

enormous role in allowing us to understand literature.  And we have not yet

even considered the "great code" of myth and metaphor.

Figure 6: How the Artist Conveys Meaning through Literature

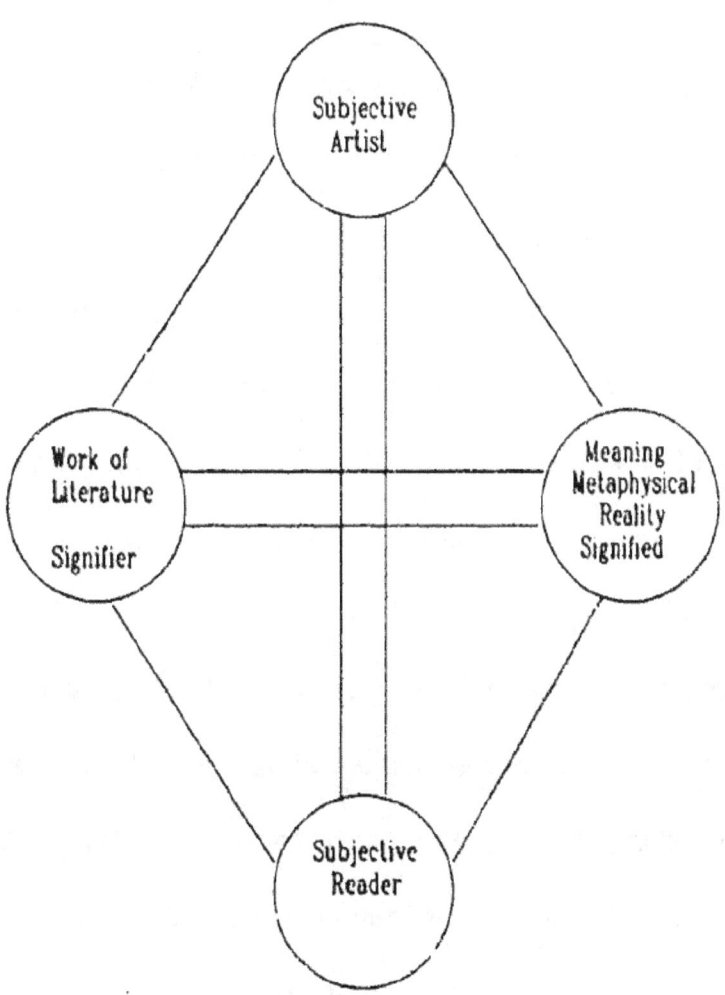

HOW ARTIST CONVEYS MEANING
TO THE READER "TRIADICALLY"

Subjective
Artist

Work of
Literature

Signifier

Meaning
Metaphysical
Reality
Signified

Subjective
Reader

## B. WHY NORTHROP FRYE'S "GREAT CODE" DOES NOT WORK

As I stated at the end of the second part of this paper, Frye was correct when he posited the "great code" of the Bible in understanding literature in typology. Having also concluded, however, that Frye's typological phase model cannot capture the meaning of Shakespeare's *Henriad*, some explanation is in order.

Frye singles out the typological connection of the Bible to literature and understands it as a metaphorical process. What makes typology so attractive in positing meaning, however, is that it is triadic. As explained earlier in this paper, when a subjective individual juxtaposes a type-antitype pair of events, a new metaphysical understanding is reached through the "vertical lift" that is "often thought of as transcending time"[278]. The relationship of the type-antitype juxtaposition with the subjective individual who experiences the vertical lift can be seen in Figure 7. The vertical lift is actually a means for the subjective individual to see beyond the individual metaphorical relationships of the type and the antitype. It opens up the typological pair to create a new and greater meaning approaching what might be called an "objective truth." As in the case of communication, the vision of this truth is only possible through the triadic relationship; it cannot be seen if the type-antitype pair is viewed causally in time.

Because typology functions triadically, whether Northrop Frye knew it or not, it is a true means through which to get at Biblical understanding. This is

Figure 7: The Triadic Nature of Typology

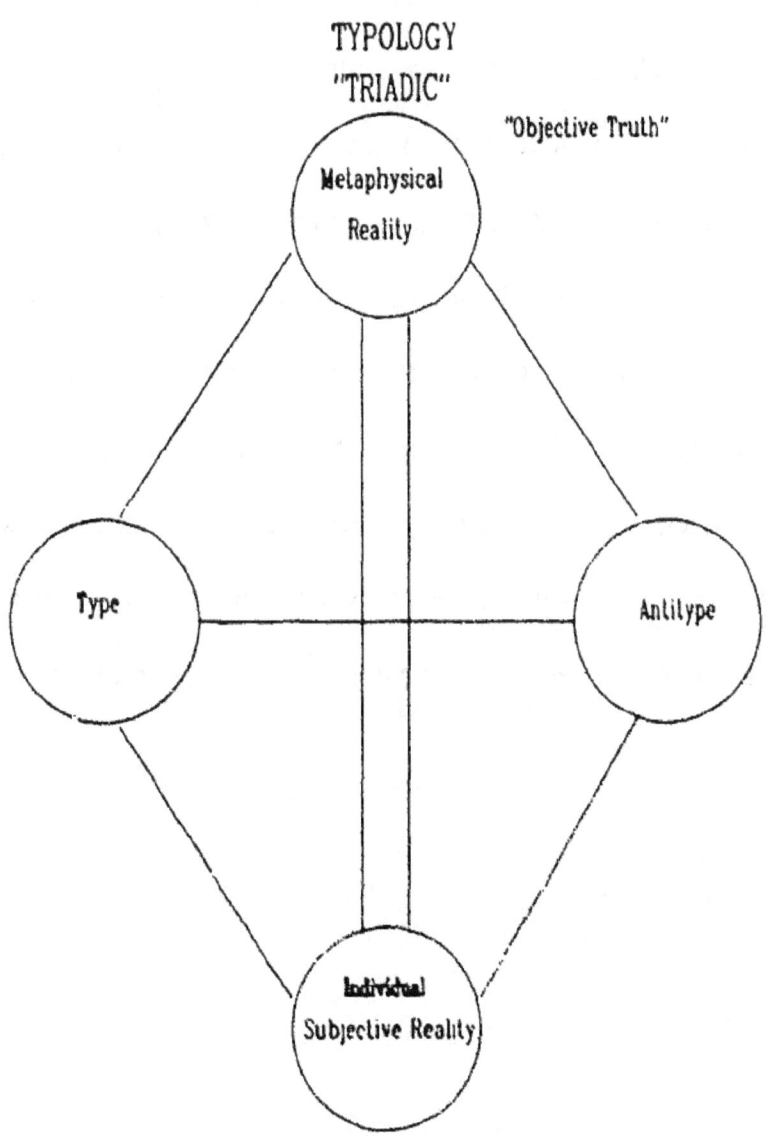

why I believe Frye was essentially correct with his analysis of typology as the "great code." Where Frye's methodology breaks down, howeve.. .s in his typological phase model. What Frye is doing with this model is applying a scientific or dyadic approach to understanding a triadic relationship. Frye's typological phase model attempts to link causally the phases of typology. In essence, the phase model is attempting to get at meaning and truth by capturing typological relationships in little boxes. Figure 8 attempts to envision graphically what Frye is doing. If the shape represents the play *Richard II*, Frye's approach can only deal with limited portions of meaning in the narrative because it must act through the royal metaphor and follow a causal sequence from type to antitype, which becomes type again and is followed by a new antitype. Each type-antitype pair then becomes a cause and an effect, being trapped in time and not allowing a vertical lift that transcends time.

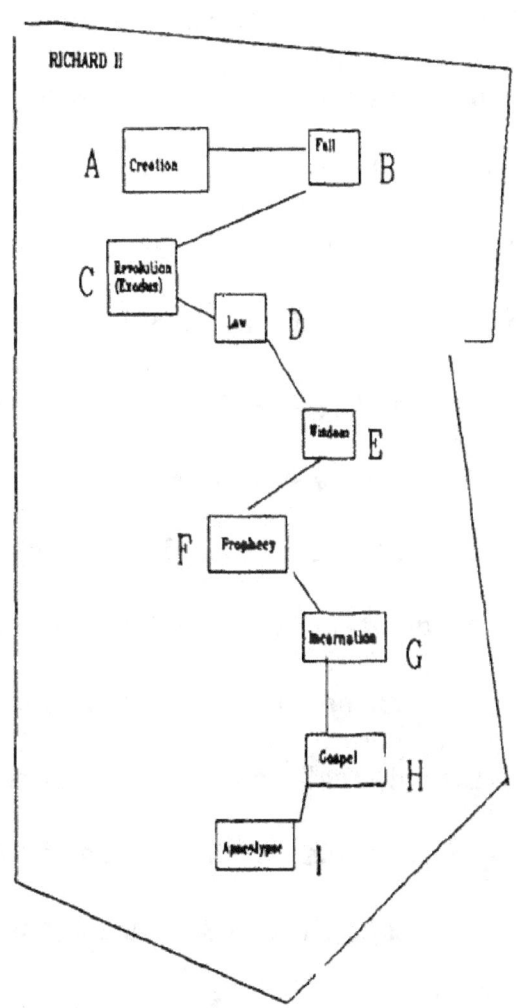

Figure 8: Why Frye's Typological Phase Model Fails

WHY NORTHROP FRYE'S TYPOLOGICAL
PHASE MODEL FAILS: CAUSAL -> "DIADIC"

## C. THE MODERN APPROACH TO LITERARY CRITICISM

Frye's dependence on a causal model is not surprising, because the field of modern literary criticism has typically taken a scientific, causal, and dyadic approach to understanding literature. Typically, modern criticism makes one of two mistakes in approaching literature, both of which are primarily causal errors. Figure 9 looks at the two "schools" of dyadic modern literary criticism.

The first of these approaches attempts to immerse itself in the reader's subjective approach to the piece of literature. The reader takes on "an exaggerated and quite unrealistic importance" in analyzing a piece of literature for meaning[279]. Because the importance of the reader (or critic) supersedes that of the literature, the literature is relegated to a mere "text" with which the reader may do as he likes. The tendency to approach a work of literature purely subjectively leads to theories on Formalism, Structuralism, Deconstruction, and even a version of Semiotics. In Formalism the critic attempts to "bracket off the actual *content* of the story and concentrate entirely on the form".[280] The Structuralist critic believes that "the individual units of any system have meaning only by virtue of their relations to one another"[281]. The "tactic" of the deconstructive critic "is to show how texts come to embrace their own ruling systems of logic"[282]. In the Semiotic approach, the critic uses one part of Saussure's semiotic theory to examine how "the relationship between signifier and signified is an arbitrary one"[283]. All of these methods, in essence, miss the point of literature in that they assume there is no meaning or "objective

Figure 9: The Dyadic Approach of Modern Literary Criticism

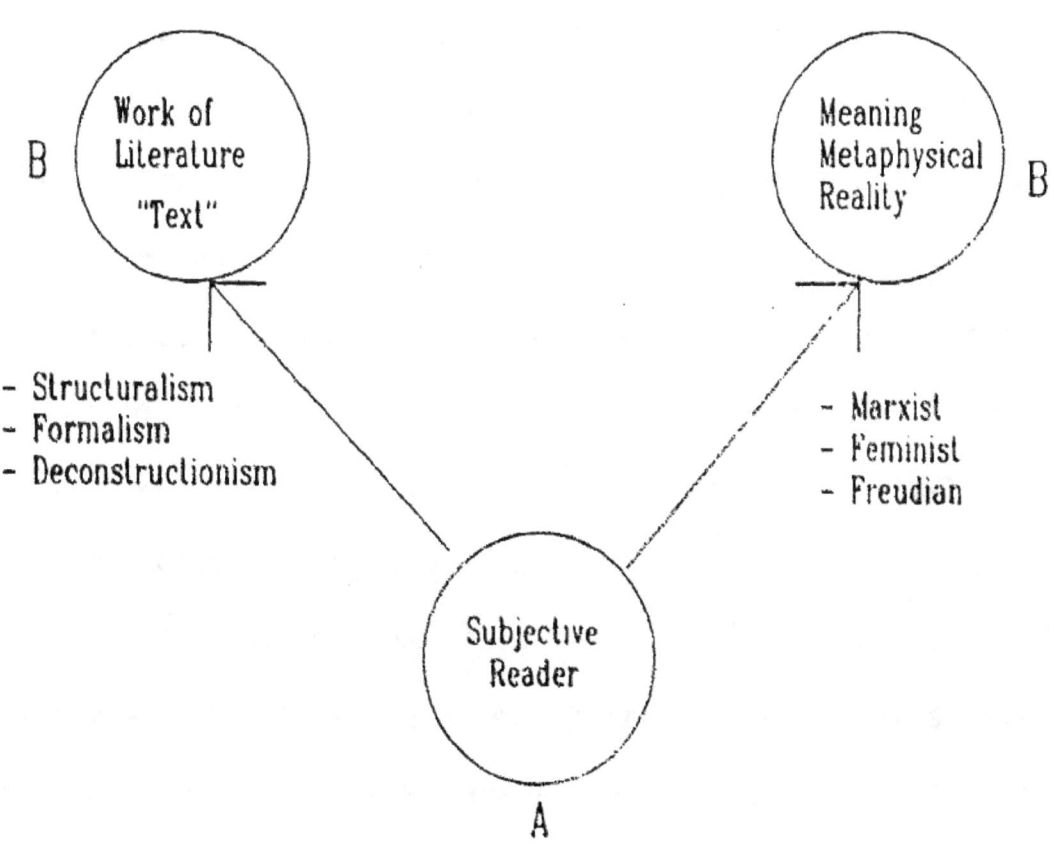

MODERN LITERARY CRITICISM'S
ATTEMPTS TO UNDERSTAND USING
A "DYADIC" APPROACH

truth" to be understood in a piece of literature. Instead they play causal games with the verbal structures of the text, getting so caught up in the signifier that they dismiss the signified. The result is an infinite number of readings that dismiss the author and any meaning that might be posited in a piece of literature.

The other approach to literature attempts to be purely objective. This game is a simple one: the literary critic believes himself superior to the work of literature and language itself, standing "in a posture of objectivity over the world" and literature[284]. The critic has a "sense of election to an elite from which vantage point [he] can play a one-upmanship game" with other critics[285]. Types of criticism in this category are the Marxist, Freudian, and feminist schools. Marxist criticism reduces literature "to the economic endeavors of individuals and classes" and the "elaborate prognosis...constructed on the theory of economic conflict and resolution"[286]. Freudian psychoanalytic criticism can attempt to interpret anything from the "psychology of the author -- or his stand-in, the character -- to that of the reader, and further to the relations between author, reader, text and language"[287]. In feminist criticism, a critic "can use whichever methods or theories she likes" that illustrate "the struggle against patriarchy and sexism"[288]. The problem with all of these methods is that they approach criticism looking for a meaning they have already determined exists in the piece of literature they are analyzing. This deterministic approach is causal and dyadic in nature and misses the subjective beauty that a work of literature can create.

Neither of these purely subjective nor objective approaches to criticism begins to understand the "truth" or "beauty" of literature. This is largely a consequence of an unbalanced and dyadic approach to literature through a fundamentally scientific critical approach. The only answer then must be in a linguistic approach to criticism that embraces both a triadic approach and balance.

## D. A TRIADIC APPROACH TO CRITICISM

One of Northrop Frye's major complaints against modern literary criticism is its "anxiety to develop criticism into a discipline that sounds linguistically mature" which "involves hitching it onto some philosophical basis"[289]. He indicates that this movement has embraced "critical approaches that move as quickly as possible into non-literary areas," misunderstanding "the very simple and primitive categories of myth and metaphor at the heart of literature"[290]. Frye does leave one avenue of future exploration open, however, that he thinks might also prove fruitful in understanding literature when he says "I am not speaking of linguistics or semiotics, where the direction is different to begin with"[291].

The basis of my exploration into a theory of language and a theory of criticism has been to pursue this avenue. The first step in this pursuit is to realize how the emphasis on criticism has changed over time. There is no better description of this process than in this excerpt from lectures Frye delivered and later published as *Creation & Recreation* (1980). Frye explains:

> For many centuries the center of gravity in literature was the hero, the man whose deeds the poet celebrated. As society slowly changed its shape, the hero modulated to the 'character' and...it was still the creation of character, as one sees it so impressively in Shakespeare, Dickens, and Browning, that was the mark of poetic power. At the same time the Romantic movement had brought with it a shift of interest from the hero to the poet himself, not merely as the creator of the hero but as the person whose inner life was the distinct from the projected subject of the poem. There resulted an extraordinary mystique of creativity, in which the artist became somehow a unique if not actually superior species of human being, with qualities of prophet, genius, wise man, and social

leader...in a short time the center of gravity in literature and critical theory would shift again, this time from the poet to the reader[292].

It is precisely this process that has created the phenomenon in modern criticism that has elevated the reader or critic to a parallel status "with the artist in a way that seems to give him an equal share at least in what the art is doing"[293]. In this way, the subjective reader is able to distort his role in the linguistic exchange that takes place in literature.

What must be kept in perspective, however, is the realization that "[e]very work of literature that we continue to study meant something to its own time" and means "something quite different to us," but that "[b]oth poles of understanding have to be kept in mind"[294]. To "disregard its original historical context, we are simply kidnapping it into the orbit of our own concerns" and to "disregard its relevance to ourselves, we are leaving it unrevealed in the morgue of the past"[295]. The solution is to keep the two meanings "together and in balance" in order to "stabiliz[e] a tradition, and...[engage] in a process which includes ourselves and yet is something bigger than ourselves"[296].

Beyond the balance that any true search for meaning in literature must employ, however, must be the realization of how literature operates. Again Frye describes it best in his introduction to *Words with Power* (1992):

> The poetic imagination constructs a cosmos of its own, a cosmos to be studied not simply as a map but as a world of powerful conflicting forces. This imaginative cosmos is neither the objective environment studied by natural causes nor a subjective inner space to be studied by psychology. It is an intermediate world in which the images of higher and lower, the

categories of beauty and ugliness, the feelings of love and hatred, the association of sense experience, can be only expressed by metaphor and yet cannot be reduced to projections of something else. Ordinary consciousness is so possessed by the either-or contrast of subject and object that it finds difficulty in taking in the notion of an order of words that is neither subjective nor objective, though it interpenetrates both. But its presence gives a very different appearance to many elements of human life, including religion, which depends on metaphor but does not become less "real" or "true" by doing so[297].

This process that Frye describes is exactly what Percy and Pierce are exploring with a triadic theory of the meaning of language. It is also what I am positing in this section on a theory of criticism. The model of criticism that I have suggested attempts to take into consideration a balanced approach to understanding literature, a triadic understanding of language, and a fundamental belief that when meaning is found using this approach it can approach an "objective truth" that is "beauty." Figure 10 illustrates this model. In this model the subjective reader reads a work of literature which is a signifier that posits a signified metaphysical reality or meaning. If the subjective reader takes a balanced approach in examining the poetry of the literature, in understanding the historical context of the work and the author, and in searching for the meaning, then the objective truth and beauty will reveal itself. The best example of this lies in the reason that criticism from centuries past maintains its popularity and pertinence: in expanding meaning, the critic was creating his own art.

Fundamentally, finding meaning in literature can be reduced to the dichotomy between embracing the existence of universals such as "beauty" and

Figure 10: A New Approach to Literary Criticism

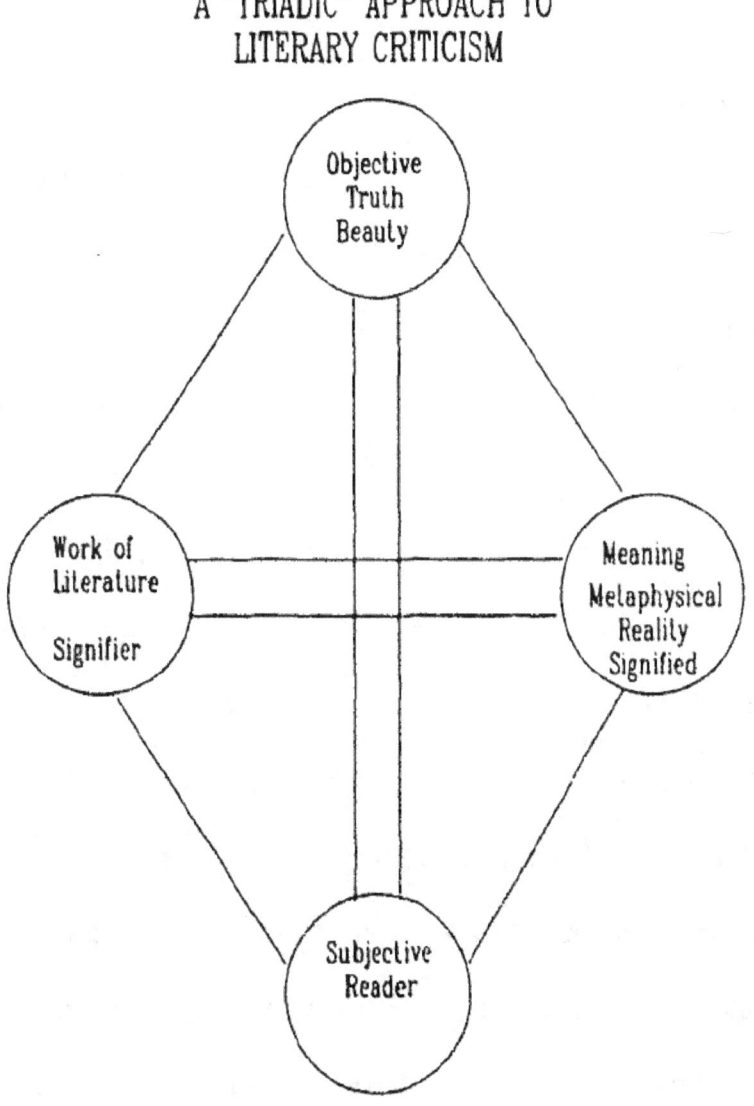

A "TRIADIC" APPROACH TO
LITERARY CRITICISM

"objective truth" or turning to "nominalism" which "denies that universals have a real existence"[298]. Again this dichotomy hinges on the difference between a scientific and linguistic understanding of the universe. The dyadic nature of scientific egoism necessarily embraces nominalism. With nominalism comes the denial of universals which "carries with it the denial of everything transcending experience" which "means inevitably...the denial of truth"[299]. "With the denial of objective truth there is no escape from the relativism of 'man the measure of all things,'" which is how the modern scientist, and the modern critic approach an understanding of the world[300].

The linguistic understanding of the world understands its own limitations. In man's fallen state, language too has fallen. Although language is the most transparent aspect of our lives, it is not a window, but a mirror as shown in Figure 11. Understanding the subjective nature of language, however, is the first step in finally seeing through it. If we realize that the nature that we can see and describe through language constitutes an "imperfect [subjective] reality," then we can use a triadic approach to meaning to catch a glimmer of the objective truth that lies just beyond the mirror. It is just behind this mirror where both the Bible and Shakespeare can be found If, however, we embrace a scientific understanding of the world, we will be forever trapped in time-bound causality that attempts objectively to analyze reality and is forever caught in the dyadic enigma of the relative meaninglessness of fact. And in this world of science, neither the Bible nor Shakespeare has any place, because both are ultimately meaningless.

**Figure 11: The Mirror of Linguistic Subjectivity**

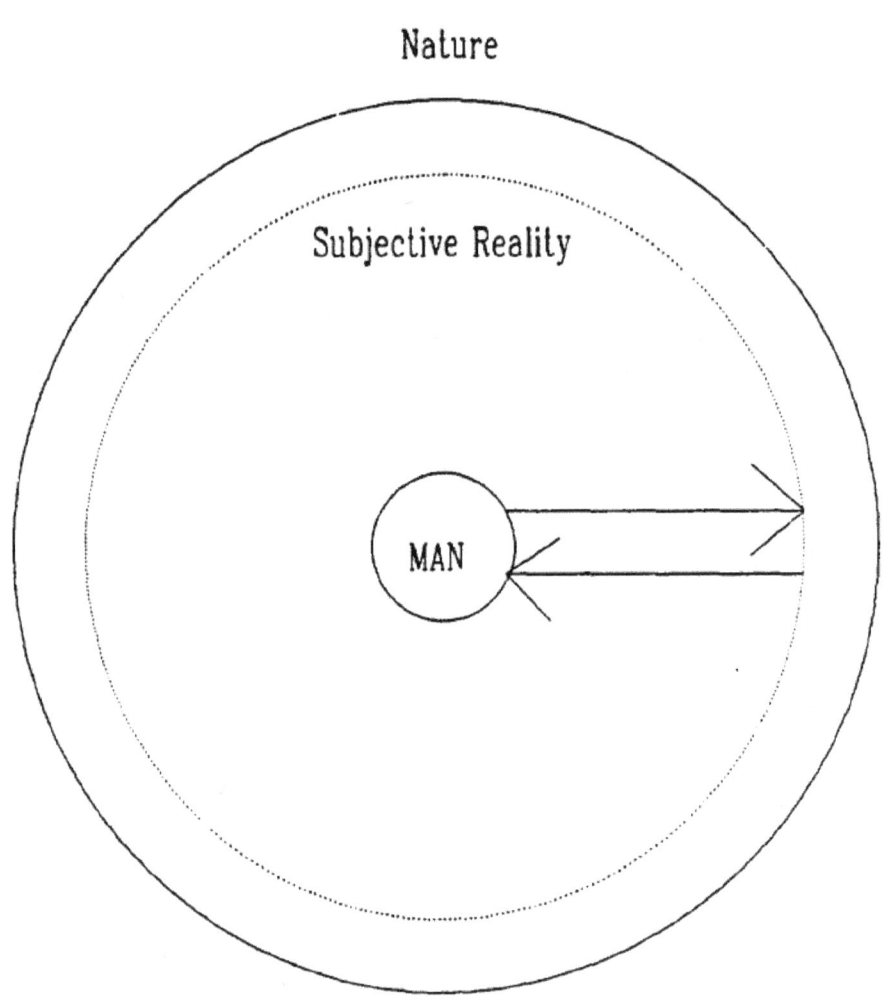

# ENDNOTES

1. Northrop Frye, *Words with Power: Being a Second Study of "The Bible and Literature"* (New York: Harcourt, Brace, Jovanovich, 1990), p. xvii.

2. Ibid., p. xii.

3. Ibid., p. xvi.

4. Ibid., p. xvi.

5. Ibid., p. xxii.

6. Peter Saccio, *Shakespeare's English Kings: History, Chronicle, and Drama* (London: Oxford University Press, 1977), pp. 39-40.

7. Ibid., pp. 43-44.

8. Ibid., p. 44.

9. *Webster's Ninth New Collegiate Dictionary* (Springfield: Merriam-Webster, 1990), p. 1268.

10. John B. Gabel and Charles B. Wheeler, *The Bible as Literature: An Introduction* (New York: Oxford University Press, 1990), p. 44 & Northrop Frye, *Words with Power: Being a Second Study of "The Bible and Literature"* (New York: Harcourt, Brace, Jovanovich, 1990), p. xxiii.

11. Edna Moore Robinson, "Shakespeare's Use of Scripture." *Biblical Images in Literature.* ed. by Roland Bartel (Nashville: Abingdon Press, 1975), p. 308.

12. Ibid., p. 308.

13. Ibid., p. 309.

14. Ibid., p. 309.

15. Ibid., p. 308.

16. Ibid., p. 309.

17. Ibid., p. 309.

18. Northrop Frye, *The Great Code: The Bible and Literature* (New York: Harcourt, Brace, Jovanovich, 1982), pp. 79-82.

19. Ibid., p. 86.

20. *Webster's Ninth New Collegiate Dictionary* (Springfield: Merriam-Webster, 1990), p. 573.

21. Northrop Frye, *Creation & Recreation* (Toronto: University of Toronto Press, 1980), p. 59.

22. Ibid., 59.

23. Northrop Frye, *The Great Code: The Bible and Literature* (New York: Harcourt, Brace, Jovanovich, 1982), p. 106.

24. Ibid., pp. 79-80, 106.

25. Northrop Frye, *Words with Power: Being a Second Study of "The Bible and Literature"* (New York: Harcourt, Brace, Jovanovich, 1990), p. xi.

26. Ibid., pp. xiii-xix.

27. Ibid., p. xviii.

28. Ibid., p. xxi.

29. Northrop Frye, *Creation & Recreation* (Toronto: University of Toronto Press, 1980), p. 64.

30. Northrop Frye, *Words with Power: Being a Second Study of "The Bible and Literature"* (New York: Harcourt, Brace, Jovanovich, 1990), p. xxi & *The Great Code: The Bible and Literature* (New York: Harcourt, Brace, Jovanovich, 1982), p. xiii.

31. David Bevington, *The Complete Works of Shakespeare*, fourth ed. (New York: HarperCollins, 1992), p. ciii.

32. Ibid., p. ciii.

33. Northrop Frye, *Words with Power: Being a Second Study of "The Bible and Literature"* (New York: Harcourt, Brace, Jovanovich, 1990), p. xx.

34. David Bevington, *The Complete Works of Shakespeare*, fourth ed. (New York: HarperCollins, 1992), p. cv.

35. Ibid., p. cv.

36. Walker Percy, "The Delta Factor," *The Message in the Bottle: How Queer Man Is, How Queer Language Is, and What One Has to Do with the Other* (New York: Noonday, 1992), pp. 3-45.

37. Walker Percy, *Lost in the Cosmos: The Last Self-Help Book*, (New York: Noonday, 1983), pp. 85-125 & Northrop Frye, *Words With Power: Being a Second Study of "The Bible and Literature"* (New York: Harcourt, Brace, Jovanovich, 1990), p. xxi.

38. Northrop Frye, *Words with Power: Being a Second Study of "The Bible and Literature"* (New York: Harcourt, Brace, Jovanovich, 1990), p. xxiii.

39.  Specific authorship and editorial problems with the First Folio and subsequent editions are nicely summarized in David Bevington's *The Complete Works of Shakespeare*, forth edition (HarperCollins, 1980) pp. lxxxiv-xciv. The main concern about these early editions was that the manuscripts that the printer received was often not one of the "good quartos" of the plays that was "based generally on Shakespeare's own drafts, or transcripts of them" (Bevington, p. lxxxix). Many "bad quartos" that had been published by some "unscrupulous bookseller to pirate an edition of a popular play" were printed in the early Folios (Bevington, p. lxxxvii).  These "bad quartos" were often based on rough copies of the play used during production known as "foul papers" (Bevington, p. lxxxiv).

   Many of the errors that occurred in these first editions of the plays were propagated by subsequent editors including Alexander Pope (Bevington, p. xcii).  By the mid-eighteenth century, subsequent editors "inevitably perpetrated more errors than [they] eliminated" from earlier editions (Bevington, p. xciii).

   The issue of which plays belonged in the canon of Shakespeare's works was also subject to debate.  The second issue of the Third Folio published in 1664 contained seven new plays: *Pericles, The London Prodigal, Thomas Lord Cromwell, Sir John Oldcastle, The Puritan, A Yorkshire Tragedy*, and *Locrine* (Bevington, p. xcii).  *Pericles* is the only one of these plays to gain acceptance as a Shakespeare original (Bevington, p. xcii).  Editors between 1664 and 1725 included these plays until Alexander Pope rejected all of them in his 1725 Edition (Bevington pp. xcii,xciii).  Edmund Malone "reintroduced *Pericles*" in 1790, after which it remained part of the canon (Bevington, p. xciii).

40.    S. Schoenbaum, *Shakespeare's Lives* (Oxford University Press, 1970), p. 529.

   Miss Bacon's book *The Philosophy of the Plays of Shakespeare Unfolded*, published in 1857, sparked the "anti-Stratfordian" movement that questioned not only the legitimate authorship of Shakespeare's plays and poetry, but ultimately his very existence (Schoenbaum, p. 529).  Rather than extol the long line of lunacy that she sparked into existence, I will dismiss this movement out of hand.

41. S. Schoenbaum, *William Shakespeare: A Compact Documentary Life* (Oxford University Press, 1977), p 12. Although the records in Stratford-upon-Avon date back to 1558 (six years before Shakespeare's birth), they are not the original records, but a copy made in the year 1600 (Schoenbaum, p. 12). Edmund Malone, a late eighteenth century Shakespearean scholar, compiled the definitive family tree for Shakespeare's father, sorting out the existence of another John Shakespeare (not Shakespeare's father) that turned up periodically (Schoenbaum, p. 13).

42. S. Schoenbaum does a meticulous job of chronicling the hundreds of biographies that have been written about Shakespeare in the 430 years since his birth in his book *Shakespeare's Lives* (Oxford University Press, 1970). The most telling aspects of this book are the "sometime opposing" views that people had of Shakespeare's life over the hundreds of years since his death and "the truth of the observation that biography tends toward oblique self-portraiture" (Schoenbaum, p. ix).

43. S. Schoenbaum, *William Shakespeare: A Compact Documentary Life* (London: Oxford University Press, 1977), pp. 24-26.

44. Ibid., p. 77.

45. Ibid., p. 296.

46. David Bevington, *The Complete Works of William Shakespeare*, fourth ed. (New York: HarperCollins,1980), p. 85.

47. Peter Milward, *Shakespeare's Religious Background* (Bloomington: Indiana University Press, 1973), p. 17.

48. Arnold Oskar Meyer, *England and the Catholic Church Under Queen Elizabeth* (London: Routledge And Kegan Paul, 1967), p. 11.

49. Ibid., p. 21.

50. Ibid., p. 309.

51. Ibid., p. 313.

52. John Henry de Groot, *The Shakespeares and "The Old Faith"* (Freeport: Books for Libraries Press, 1946), p. 111.

53. Ibid., p. 111.

54. S. Schoenbaum, *William Shakespeare: A Compact Documentary Life* (London: Oxford University Press, 1977), p. 42.

55. John Henry de Groot, *The Shakespeare and "The Old Faith"* (Freeport: Books for Libraries Press, 1946), p. 65.

56. George A. Plimpton, *The Education of Shakespeare: Illustrated from the Schoolbooks in Use in his Time* (London: Oxford University Press, 1933), p. 45.

57. John Henry de Groot, *The Shakespeare and "The Old Faith"* (Freeport: Books for Libraries Press, 1946), p. 151.

58. Ibid., p. 150.

59. Ibid., p. 150.

60. Ibid., p. 157.

61. Peter Milward, *Shakespeare's Religious Background* (Bloomington: Indiana University Press, 1973), p. 87.

62. John Henry de Groot, *The Shakespeare and "The Old Faith"* (Freeport: Books for Libraries Press), p. 111.

63. *English Mystery Plays: A Selection*, ed. Peter Happé (New York: Penguin Books, 1975), pp. 18-19.

64. Ibid., p. 19.

65. Katherine Lee Bates, *The English Religious Drama* (Port Washington: Kennikat Press, 1966), p. 41.

66. *English Mystery Plays: A selection*, ed. Peter Happé (New York: Penguin Books, 1975), p. 19 & Katherine Bates, *The English Religious Drama* (Port Washington: Kennikat Press, 1966), p. 39.

67. Katherine Bates, *The English Religious Drama* (Port Washington: Kennikat Press, 1966), p. 38.

68. *English Mystery Plays*, ed. Peter Happé (New York: Penguin Books, 1975), p. 24.

69. S. Schoenbaum, *Shakespeare: His Life, His Language, His Theater* (New York: Signet Classic, 1990), p. 66.

70. Ibid., p. 66.

71. Ibid., p. 101.

72. S. Schoenbaum, *William Shakespeare: A Compact Documentary Life* (London: Oxford University Press, 1977), p. 58 & Peter Milward, *Shakespeare's Religious Background* (Bloomington: Indiana University Press, 1973), pp. 33-4.

73. Russell Fraser, *Young Shakespeare* (New York: Columbia University Press, 1988), p. 107.

74. Ibid., p. 107.

75. Northrop Frye, *Words with Power: Being a Second Study in "the Bible and Literature"* (New York: Harcourt, Brace, Jovanovich, 1990), p. xxii.

76. Northrop Frye, *The Great Code: The Bible and Literature* (New York: Harcourt, Brace, Jovanovich, 1982), p. 78.

77. Ibid., p. 79.

78. John B. Gabel and Charles B. Wheeler, *The Bible as Literature: An Introduction* (New York: Oxford University Press, 1990), p. 258.

79. Northrop Frye, *The Great Code: The Bible and Literature* (New York: Harcourt, Brace, Jovanovich, 1982), p. 79.

80. Ibid., p. 79.

81. Ibid., p. 79.

82. Northrop Frye, *Creation & Recreation* (Toronto: Univarsity of Toronto Press, 1980), p. 59.

83. Northrop Frye, *The Great Code: The Bible and Literature* (New York: Harcourt, Brace, Jovanovich), pp. 79-80.

84. Ibid., p. 53.

85. Northrop Frye, *Words with Power: Being a Second Study of "The Bible and Literature"* (New York: Harcourt, Brace, Jovanovich, 1990), p. xvi.

86. Ibid., p. xii.

87. Ibid., p. xiii.

88. Ibid., p. xiv.

89. Northrop Frye, *The Great Code: The Bible and Literature* (New York: Harcourt, Brace, Jovanovich, 1982), pp xii-xiii.

90. Ibid., p. xi.

91. Northrop Frye, *Creation & Recreation* (Toronto: University of Toronto Press, 1980), p. 4.

92. Northrop Frye, *The Great Code: The Bible and Literature* (Harcourt, Brace, Jovanovich, 1982), p. 106.

93. Ibid., p. xi.

94. Northrop Frye, *Creation & Recreation* (Toronto: University of Toronto Press, 1980), p. 4.

95. Ibid., p. 7.

96. Ibid., p. 7.

97. Ibid., p. 7.

98. Ibid., p. 7.

99. Ibid., p. 7.

100. Ibid., pp. 7,5.

101. Ibid., p. 13.

102. Ibid., p. 13.

103. Northrop Frye, *Words with Power: Being a Second Study in "The Bible and Literature"* (Harcourt, Brace, Jovanovich, 1990), p. xv.

104. Ibid., p. xv.

105. Northrop Frye, *Creation & Recreation* (Toronto: University of Toronto Press, 1980), p. 3.

106. John B. Gabel and Charles B. Wheeler, *The Bible as Literature: An Introduction* (New York: Oxford University Press, 1990), pp. 43,44.

107. Northrop Frye, *Creation & Recreation* (Toronto: University of Toronto Press, 1980), p. 58.

108. Ibid., p. 59.

109. Ibid., p. 59.

110. Northrop Frye, *The Great Code: The Bible and Literature* (Harcourt, Brace, Jovanovich, 1982), p. 82.

111. Ibid., pp. 80-1.

112. Northrop Frye, *Creation & Recreation* (Toronto: University of Toronto Press, 1980), p. 59.

113. Northrop Frye, *The Great Code: The Bible and Literature* (New York: Harcourt, Brace, Jovanovich, 1982), p. 80.

114. Ibid., p. 81.

115. Ibid., p. 81.

116. Ibid., p. 81.

117. Ibid., p. 82.

118. Ibid., p. 81.

119. Ibid., p. 81.

120. Ibid., p. 81.

121. Northrop Frye, *Creation & Recreation* (Toronto: University of Toronto Press, 1980), p. 59.

122. Northrop Frye, *The Great Code: the Bible and Literature* (New York: Harcourt, Brace, Jovanovich, 1982), p. 81.

123. Ibid., p. 81.

124. Ibid., p. 82.

125. Ibid., pp. 81-82,82.

126. Ibid., p. 82.

127. Northrop Frye, *Creation & Recreation* (Toronto: University of Toronto Press, 1980), p 59.

128. Northrop Frye, *The Great Code: The Bible and Literature* (New York: Harcourt, Brace. Jovanovich, 1982), p. 81.

129. Northrop Frye, *Creation & Recreation* (Toronto: University of Toronto Press, 1980), p. 60.

130. E.M. Tillyard, *Shakespeare's History Plays* (London: Chatto & Windus, 1944), p. 9.

131. Northrop Frye, *Creation & Recreation* (Toronto: University of Toronto Press, 1980), p. 53.

132. Northrop Frye, *The Great Code: The Bible and Literature* (New York: Harcourt, Brace, Jovanovich, 1982), p. 85.

133. Ibid., p. 82.

134. Northrop Frye, *Creation & Recreation* (Toronto: University of Toronto Press, 1980), p. 59.

135. J.A. Bryant, Jr., *Hippolyta's View: Some Christian Aspects of Shakespeare's Plays* (University of Kentucky Press, 1961) & Northrop Frye, *Creation & Recreation* (Toronto: University of Toronto Press, 1980), p. 59.

136. Northrop Frye, *Creation & Recreation* (Toronto: University of Toronto Press, 1980), pp. 59-60.

137. Ibid., p. 60.

138. Ibid., p. 60.

139. Ibid., p. 60.

140. Ibid., p. 60.

141. Northrop Frye, *Creation & Recreation* (Toronto: University of Toronto Press, 1980), p. 60.

142. Northrop Frye, *Creation & Recreation* (Toronto: University of Toronto Press, 1980), p. 61.

143. Northrop Frye, *The Great Code: The Bible and Literature* (New York: Harcourt, Brace, Jovanovich, 1982), p. 83.

144. Northrop Frye, *Creation & Recreation* (Toronto: University of Toronto Press, 1980), p. 61.

145. Northrop Frye, *The Great Code: The Bible and Literature* (New York: Harcourt, Brace, Jovanovich, 1982), p. 83.

146. Ibid., p. 83.

147. Northrop Frye, *The Great Code: The Bible and Literature* (New York: Harcourt, Brace, Jovanovich, 1982), p. 83 & Northrop Frye, *Creation & Recreation* (Toronto: University of Toronto Press, 1980), p. 61.

148. Northrop Frye, *Creation & Recreation* (Toronto: University of Toronto Press, 1980), p. 60.

149. John B. Gabel and Charles B. Wheeler, *The Bible as Literature: An Introduction* (New York: Oxford University Press, 1990), p. 45.

150. Northrop Frye, *Creation & Recreation* (Toronto: University of Toronto Press, 1980), p. 45.

151. Northrop Frye, *Words with Power: Being a Second Study in "The Bible and Literature"* (New York: Harcourt, Brace, Jovanovich, 1982), p. xvi.

152. Ibid., p. xvi.

153. Northrop Frye, *The Great Code: The Bible and Literature* (New York: Harcourt, Brace, Jovanovich, 1982), p. 106.

154. Ibid., p. 106.

155. Ibid., p. 106.

156. Ibid., p. 106.

157. Ibid., p. 106.

158. Ibid., p. 106.

159. Ibid., p. 109.

160. Ibid., pp. 128, 129.

161. Ibid., p. 106.

162. Ibid., p. 106.

163. Ibid., p. 106.

164. Northrop Frye, *Creation & Recreation* (Toronto: University of Toronto Press, 1980), p. 34.

165. Ibid., p. 34.

166. Northrop Frye, *The Great Code: The Bible and Literature* (New York: Harcourt, Brace, Jovanovich, 1982), p. 109.

167. Northrop Frye, *Creation & Recreation* (Toronto: University of Toronto Press, 1980), p. 37.

168. Northrop Frye, *The Great Code: The Bible and Literature* (New York: Harcourt, Brace, Jovanovich, 1982), p. 107.

169. Ibid., p. 108.

170. Northrop Frye, *Creation & Recreation* (Toronto: University of Toronto Press, 1980), p. Northrop Frye, *The Great Code: The Bible and Literature* (New York: Harcourt, Brace, Jovanovich, 1982), p. 109.

171. Northrop Frye, *The Great Code: The Bible and Literature* (New York: Harcourt, Brace, Jovanovich, 1982), p. 110.

172. Northrop Frye, *Creation & Recreation* (Toronto: University of Toronto Press, 1980), p. 33.

173. Northrop Frye, *The Great Code: The Bible and Literature* (New York: Harcourt, Brace, Jovanovich, 1982), p. 110.

174. Northrop Frye, *Creation & Recreation* (Toronto: University of Toronto Press, 1980), p. 35.

175. Northrop Frye, *The Great Code: The Bible and Literature* (New York: Harcourt, Brace, Jovanovich, 1982), p. 148.

176. Northrop Frye, *Creation & Recreation* (Toronto: University of Toronto Press, 1980), p. 53, Northrop Frye, *The Great Code: The Bible and Literature* (New York: Harcourt, Brace, Jovanovich, 1982), p. 110.

177. Northrop Frye, *The Great Code: The Bible and Literature* (New York: Harcourt, Brace, Jovanovich, 1982), p. 114.

178. Ibid., p. 115.

179. Ibid., p. 116.

180. Ibid., p. 117.

181. Ibid., p. 117.

182. Ibid., p. 117.

183. Ibid., p. 118.

184. Ibid., p. 118.

185. Ibid., pp. 119,120.

186. Ibid., p. 121.

187. Ibid., p. 121.

188. Ibid., pp. 121,125.

189. Ibid., p. 121.

190. Ibid., p. 128.

191. Ibid., p. 129.

192. Ibid., p. 125.

193. Ibid., p. 128.

194. Ibid., p. 128.

195. Ibid., p. 129.

196. Ibid., p. 129.

197. Ibid., p. 98.

198. Northrop Frye, *Creation & Recreation* (Toronto: University of Toronto Press, 1980), p. 39.

199. Northrop Frye, *The Great Code: The Bible and Literature* (New York: Harcourt, Brace, Jovanovich, 1982), p. 129.

200. Northrop Frye, *Creation & Recreation* (Toronto: University of Toronto Press, 1980), p. 129.

201. Northrop Frye, *The Great Code: The Bible and Literature* (New York: Harcourt, Brace, Jovanovich, 1982), p. 129.

202. Ibid., p. 129.

203. Ibid., p. 130.

204. Ibid., p. 130.

205. Ibid., p. 130.

206. Ibid., p. 130.

207. Ibid., p. 130.

208. Ibid., p. 131.

209. Ibid., p. 131.

210. Ibid., p. 132.

211. Ibid., pp. 133,134.

212. Ibid., p. 135.

213. Ibid., p. 135.

214. Ibid., pp. 135-6.

215. Ibid., p. 136.

216. Ibid., p. 136.

217. Ibid., p. 136.

218. Ibid., p. 136.

219. Ibid., p. 136.

220. Ibid., p. 136.

221. Ibid., p. 137.

222. Ibid., p. xvii.

223. Ibid., p. xiii.

224. John Wilders, *The Lost Garden: A View of Shakespeare's English and Roman History Plays* (Totowa: Rowman and Littlefield, 1978).

225. Lily B. Campbell, *Shakespeare's "Histories": Mirror of Elizabethan Policy* (London: University Paperbacks, 1970), p. 12.

226. Northrop Frye, *The Great Code: The Bible and Literature* (New York: Harcourt, Brace, Jovanovich, 1982), p. 87.

227. Ibid., p. 86.

228. Ibid., p. 90.

229. Ibid., p. 99.

230. Ibid., p. 109.

231. Ibid., p. 114.

232. Ibid., p. 130.

233. Ibid., p. 133.

234. Ibid., p. 114.

235. Ibid., p. 135.

236. Ibid., p. 114.

237. Ibid., p. 115.

238. Ibid., p. 117.

239. ibid., p. 98.

240. Ibid., p. 136.

241. Ibid., p. 136.

242. Ibid., p. 135.

243. Ibid., p. 137.

244. Walker Percy, *Lost in the Cosmos: The Last Self-Help Book* (New York: Noonday, 1983), p. 85.

245. Ibid., p. 85.

246. Ibid., p. 85.

247. Northrop Frye, *Creation & Recreation* (Toronto: University of Toronto Press, 1980), pp. 6-7.

248. Ibid., p. 27.

249. Walker Percy, *Lost in the Cosmos: The Last Self-Help Book* (New York: Noonday,1983), p. 87.

250. Northrop Frye, *Creation & Recreation* (Toronto: University of Toronto Press, 1980), p. 59.

251. Ibid., p. 7.

252. Walker Percy, "A Triadic Theory of Meaning," *The Message in the Bottle: How Queer Man Is, How Queer Language Is, and What One Has To Do With the Other* (New York: Noonday, 1992), p. 161.

253. Ibid., p. 116.

254. Ibid., pp. 162, 161.

255. Ibid., p. 162.

256. Northrop Frye, *Creation & Recreation* (Toronto: University of Toronto Press, 1980), p. 59.

257. Charles S. Peirce, *Philosophical Writings of Peirce* (New York: Dover Publications, 1955), p. 90.

258. Ernest Nagal, *The Structure of Science: Problems in the Logic of Scientific Exploration* (New York: Harcourt, Brace & World, 1961), p. 319.

259. Walker Percy, "A Triadic Theory of Meaning," *The Message in the Bottle: How Queer Man Is, How Queer Language Is, and What One Has To Do With the Other* (New York: Noonday, 1992), p. 162.

260. Ibid., p. 162.

261. David Halliday and Robert Resnick, *Physics: For Students of Science and Engineering* (New York: John Wiley & Sons, 1962), p. 1119.

262. Ernest Nagal, *The Structure of Science: Problems in the Logic of Scientific Exploration* (New York: Harcourt, Brace & World, 1961), p. 227.

263. Ibid., p. 297.

264. Walker Percy, "A Triadic Theory of Meaning," *The Message in the Bottle: How Queer Man Is, How Queer Language Is, and What One Has To Do With the Other* (New York: Noonday, 1992), p. 161.

265. Ibid., p. 161.

266. Ibid., p. 161.

267. Charles S. Peirce, *Philosophical Writings of Peirce* (New York: Dover Publications, 1955), p. 91.

268. Walker Percy, *Lost in the Cosmos: The Last Self-Help Book* (New York: Noonday, 1983), p. 103.

269. Ibid., p. 103.

270. Northrop Frye, *Creation & Recreation* (Toronto: University of Toronto Press, 1980) p. 67.

271. Ibid., p. 70.

272. Richard M. Weaver, *Ideas Have Consequences* (Chicago: University of Chicago, 1957), p. 58.

273. Ibid., p. 148.

274. Ibid., pp. 152,148.

275. Ibid., p. 152.

276. Northrop Frye, *Creation & Recreation* (Toronto: University of Toronto Press, 1980), p. 67.

277. Ibid., p. 4.

278. Northrop Frye, *The Great Code: The Bible and Literature* (New York: Harcourt, Brace, Jovanovich, 1982), p. 82.

279. Northrop Frye, *Creation & Recreation* (Toronto: University of Toronto Press, 1980), p. 64.

280. Terry Eagleton, *Literary Theory: An Introduction* (Minneapolis: University of Minnesota Press, 1983), p. 95.

281. Ibid., p. 94.

282. Ibid., p. 133.

283. Ibid., p. 97.

284. Walker Percy, *Lost in the Cosmos: The Last Self-Help Book* (New York: Noonday, 1983), p. 115.

285. Ibid., p. 117.

286. Richard M. Weaver, *Ideas Have Consequences* (Chicago: University of Chicago, 1957), p. 6.

287. Elizabeth Wright, "Modern Psychoanalytic Criticism," *Modern Literary Theory: A Comparative Introduction*, ed. Ann Jefferson and David Robey (London: B.T. Batsford, 1982), p. 145.

288. Toril Moi, "Feminist Literary Criticism," *Modern Literary Theory: A Comparative Introduction*, ed. Ann Jefferson and David Robey (London: B.T. Batsford, 1982), p. 204.

289. Northrop Frye, *Words with Power: Being a Second Study in "The Bible and Literature"* (New York: Harcourt, Brace, Jovanovich, 1982), pp. xvi-xvii.

290. Ibid., p. xvii.

291. Ibid., p. xvii.

292. Northrop Frye, *Creation & Recreation* (Toronto: University of Toronto Press, 1980), p. 64.

293. Ibid., p. 60.

294. Ibid., p. 67.

295. Ibid., p. 67.

296. Ibid., p. 67.

297. Northrop Frye, *Words with Power: Being a Second Study in "The Bible and Literature"* (New York: Harcourt, Brace, Jovanovich, 1982), pp. xxii-xiii.

298. Richard M. Weaver, *Ideas Have Consequences* (Chicago: University of Chicago, 1957), p. 3.

299. Ibid., p. 4.

300. Ibid., p. 4.

# BIBLIOGRAPHY

Baldwin, T. W.
*Shakespeare's Small Latine & Lesse Greeke*
Urbana, III., 1944

Baldwin, T. W.
*William Shakespeare's Petty School*
Urbana, III., 1943

Bates, Katharine Lee
*The English Religious Drama*
Port Washington: Kennikat Press, 1966

Bartel, Roland ed.
*Biblical Images in Literature*
Nashville: Abingdon Press, 1975

Bevington, David
*The Complete Works of Shakespeare*, fourth ed.
New York: HarperCollins, 1992

Birt, Henry Nobert
*The Elizabethan Religious Settlement; A Study of Contemporary Documents*
London: G. Bell, 1907

Bloom, Harold
*Shakespeare's Histories*
New York: Chelsea House Publishers, 1986
book of essays

Brawley, Benjamin
*A Short History of English Drama*
Freeport: Books For Libraries Press, 1969

Bryant, J.A. Jr.
*Hippolyta's View: Some Christian Aspects of Shakespeare's Plays*
University of Kentucky Press, 1960

Byrne M. St. Clare
*Elizabethan Life in Town and Country*
New York: Houghton Mifflin Company, 1926

Campbell, Lily B.
*Shakespeare's Histories*
London, Butler & Tanner Ltd., 1964

Curry, Walter Clyde
*Shakespeare's Philosophical Patterns*
Baton Rouge: Louisiana State University Press, 1959

Davidson, Clifford
*Studies in the English Mystery Plays*
New York: Haskell House, 1965

de Groot, John Henry
*The Shakespeare and the Old Faith*
Freeport: Books for Libraries Press, 1968

Eagleton, Terry
*Literary Theory: An Introduction*
Minneapolis, University of Minnesota Press, 1983

Fraser, Russell A.
*Young Shakespeare*
New York: Columbia University Press, 1988

Frye, Northrop
*Anatomy of Criticism*
Princeton: Princeton University Press, 1957

Frye, Northrop
*Creation & Recreation*
Toronto: University of Toronto Press, 1980

Frye, Northrop
*The Great Code: the Bible and Literature*
New York: Harcourt, Brace, Jovanovich, 1982

Frye, Northrop (ed. by Robert Sandler)
*On Shakespeare*
New Haven: Yale University Press, 1986

Frye, Northrop
*Words with Power: Being a Second Study of "The Bible and Literature"*
New York: Harcourt, Brace, Jovanovich, 1990

Frye, Roland Mushat
*The Art of the Dramatist*
London: Allen & Unwin, 1982

Frye, Roland Mushat
*Shakespeare & Christian Doctrine*
Princeton: Princeton University Press, 1963

Gable, John B & Wheeler, Charles B.
*The Bible as Literature*
London: Oxford University Press, 1990

Gee, Henry
*The Elizabethan Clergy and the Settlement of Religion, 1558-1564*
Oxford: The Claredon Press, 1898

Halliday, David
*Physics*
New York, John Wiley and Sons, 1962

Happé, Peter, ed.
*English Mystery Plays*
New York: Penguin Books, 1975

Kahrl, Stanley J.
*Traditions of Medieval Drama*
London: Hutchinson University Library, 1974

Jefferson, Ann
*Modern Literary Theory: A Comparative Introduction*
London: B. T. Batsford, 1982

Laroque, Francois
*Shakespeare's Festive World: Elizabethan Seasonal Entertainment and the Professional Stage*
Cambridge: Cambridge University Press, 1991

Lee, Sidney, Sir
*A Life of William Shakespeare*
New York: The Macmillan Company, 1916.

Levi, Peter
*The Life and Times of William Shakespeare*
New York: Henry Holt and Company, 1988

Lovejoy, Arthur O
*The Great Chain of Being; a Study of the History of an Idea*
Cambridge, Mass.: Harvard University Press, 1961

Ludowky, E.F.C.
*Understanding Shakespeare*
Cambridge: Cambridge University Press, 1964

Meyer, Arnold Oskar
*England and the Catholic Church Under Queen Elizabeth*
London: Routledge and Kegan Paul, 1967

Milward, Peter.
*Shakespeare's Religious Background*
Bloomington: Indiana University Press, 1973

Nagal, Earnest
*The Structure of Science: Problems in the Logic of Scientific Exploration*
New York: Harcourt Brace and World, 1961

Nelson, Alan H.
*The Medieval English Stage*
Chicago: University of Chicago Press, 1974

Nicoll, Allardyce
*The Elizabethans*
Cambridge: Cambridge University Press, 1957

Nicoll, Allardyce & Josephine
*Holinshed Chronicle, as Used in Shakespeare's Plays*
New York: Dutton, 1927

Noble, Richmond
*Shakespeare's Biblical Knowledge and Use of the Book of Common Prayer, as Exemplified by the Plays of the First Folio*
New York: Octagon Books, 1970

Pearlman, E.
*William Shakespeare: The History Plays*
New York: Maxwell Macmillan International, 1992.

Charles S. Pierce
*Philosophical Writings*
New York: Dover Publications, 1955

Percy, Walker
*Lost in the Cosmos*
New York: Noonday, 1983

Percy, Walker
*The Message in the Bottle*
New York: Noonday, 1992

Percy, Walker
*Signposts in a Strange Land*
New York: Noonday, 1991

Plimpton, George Arthur
*The Education of Shakespeare Illustrated from the Schoolbooks in Use in his
Time*
London: Oxford University Press, 1933

Prosser, Eleanor
*Drama and Religion in the English Mystery Plays,*
Stanford: Stanford University Press, 1961

Reese, M.M.
*Shakespeare, his World & his Work*
New York: St. Martin's Press, 1953

Ribner, Irving
*The English History play in the Age of Shakespeare*
Princeton: Princeton University Press, 1957

Roston, Mary
*Biblical Drama in England*
Evanston: Northwestern University Press, 1968

Rowse, A.L.
*Shakespeare the Elizabethan*
New York: Putnam, 1977

Rowse, A.L.
*William Shakespeare: A Biography*
New York: Harper & Row Publishers, 1963

Saccio, Peter
*Shakespeare's English Kings: History, Chronicle, Drama*
London: Oxford University Press, 1977

Schoenbaum S.
*Internal Evidence and Elizabethan Dramatic Authorship: An Essay in Literary History and Method*
Evanston: Northwestern University Press, 1966

Schoenbaum, S.
*Shakespeare: His Life, His Language, His Theater*
New York: Penguin Group, 1990

Schoenbaum, S.
*Shakespeare's Lives*
New York: Oxford University Press, 1970

Schoenbaum, S.
*William Shakespeare, a Compact Documentary Life*
New York: Oxford University Press, 1977

Shaheen, Naseeb
*Biblical References in Shakespeare's History Plays*
Newark: University of Delaware Press, 1989

Symonds, John Addington
*Shakespeare's Predecessors in the English Drama*
New York: Cooper Square Publishers, 1967

Tillyard, E.M.W.
*The Elizabethan World Picture*
New York: The Macmillan Company, 1944

Tillyard, E.M.W.
*Shakespeare's History Plays*
London: Chatto & Windus, 1980

Traversi, D.A.
*An Approach to Shakespeare*
Garden City: Doubleday & Company, Inc., 1956

Traversi, Derek Antona
*Shakespeare, from Richard II to Henry V*
Stanford, Calif., Stanford University Press, 1957.

Travis, Peter W.
*Dramatic Design in the Chester Cycle*
Chicago: University of Chicago Press, 1982

Weaver, Richard M.
*Ideas Have Consequences*
Chicago: University of Chicago Press, 1948

Wickham, Glynne
*The Medieval Theater*
Cambridge: Cambridge University Press, 1987

Wilders, John
*The Lost Garden: A View of Shakespeare's English and Roman History Plays*
Totowa: Rowman and Littlefield, 1987

Williams, Arnold
*Drama of Medieval England*
East Lansing: Michigan State University Press, 1961

Woolf, Rosemary
*The English Mystery Play*
London: Routledge and Kegan Paul, 1972

Wordsworth, Charles
*Shakespeare's Knowledge and Use of the Bible.*
New York: AMS Press, 1973

www.ingramcontent.com/pod-product-compliance
Lightning Source LLC
Chambersburg PA
CBHW081214280526
45787CB00006B/2405